The Early  Safety
Handbook

The layout and presentation of the text, with bullet points, checklists and sample policy documents make the book useful for staff training sessions as well as a reference point for practitioners with management responsibility for any aspect of early years practice.

Early Years Update

If you work in early years settings it is essential that you are well informed and aware of health and safety issues and procedures that you may face on a day-to-day basis. Building on the author's previous books *How to Keep Children Safe* and *How to do a Health and Safety Audit*, this book offers clear, concise and practical information about health and safety, whilst fully translating the legislative documentation that surrounds it to ensure that you meet the statutory requirements of the Early Years Foundation Stage.

Each chapter includes a summary of key points, self review activities and best practice checklists to help you apply the information to everyday activities. There are also clear guidelines on how to carry out a health and safety audit along with photocopiable templates and forms that can be easily adapted for your own use. Covering all aspects of health and safety, *The Early Years Health and Safety Handbook* includes guidance on issues such as:

- planning for a safe environment;
- risk assessments;
- the most common types of accidents and how to prevent them;
- safety for indoor and outdoor play;
- preparing for outings and trips;
- first aid for staff and children.

Written in accordance with national health and safety standards that have to be achieved at inspection, this 'how to' guide is vital for anyone working in an early years setting looking to certify that their environment is safe as well as fun.

Lynn Parker is a qualified nurse specialist with over 20 years' experience and co-founder of *Healthcare A2Z*, a company that provides web-based information, education and resources for healthcare professionals.

The Early Years Health and Safety Handbook

Lynn Parker

 Routledge
Taylor & Francis Group

LONDON AND NEW YORK

First published 2006 as *How to Do a Health and Safety Audit* and *How to Keep Young Children Safe* by David Fulton Publishers

This edition published 2012
by Routledge
2 Park Square, Milton Park, Abingdon, Oxon OX14 4RN

Simultaneously published in the USA and Canada
by Routledge
711 Third Avenue, New York, NY 10017

Routledge is an imprint of the Taylor & Francis Group, an informa business

British Library Cataloguing in Publication Data
A catalogue record for this book is available from the British Library

Library of Congress Cataloging in Publication Data
Parker, Lynn.
The early years health and safety handbook / Lynn Parker. — 2nd ed.
p. cm.
Includes bibliographical references and index.
1. School children—Health and hygiene—Handbooks, manuals, etc. 2. Early childhood education—Handbooks, manuals, etc. 3. School health services—Handbooks, manuals, etc. 4. Schools—Safety measures—Handbooks, manuals, etc. 5. Schools—Security measures—Handbooks, manuals, etc. 6. Day care centers—Health aspects—Handbooks, manuals, etc. 7. Day care centers—Safety measures—Handbooks, manuals, etc. I. Title.
LB3405.P37 2012
371.7'1—dc23

ISBN: 978-0-415-67532-1 (pbk)
ISBN: 978-0-203-80966-2 (ebk)

Typeset in Helvetica
by FiSH Books, Enfield

Printed and bound in Great Britain by the MPG Books Group

Contents

Acknowledgements

I would like to acknowledge and offer my thanks to the following people who have supported me through the writing of this book.

To the Little Owls Day Care at the Nene School, for allowing me to use their photographs of the inside activity areas.

To Sawtry Day Nursery for allowing me to take photographs of their outside activity area and to use them in this book.

To Patricia Higham for providing her expert knowledge in this area of childcare and her support and encouragement in bringing this second edition to completion.

Finally I would like to thank Annamarie Kino and James Hobbs at Routledge for guiding me through the publishing process.

1 Planning for safety

Introduction

Children are naturally curious and need constant supervision. This is why it is important to assess your setting for risks and to incorporate safety features into your structure, policies and practice. When considering both inside and outside spaces it is important to think of the activities that will be undertaken there. Whilst most accidents that happen to young children occur in and around the home, accidents can and do happen to children in early years settings. Children experience minor injuries every day, ranging from scratches to bumps and bruises. Most injuries of the minor or indeed more serious type are the result of falls, burns, scalds, poisoning and near drowning. Planning for safety means that everyone has to be involved – including parents and the children themselves. This chapter provides a template for a suggested safety plan, a self review activity and a checklist of best practice to consider.

Appointing a safety worker

Under the *Health and Safety at Work etc. Act 1974* everyone has a responsibility to maintain a safe working environment but there should be one person with overall responsibility for co-ordinating and making sure that it happens. It is important to be clear about who will manage this responsibility when the named worker is on holiday or off sick.

Even the smallest of early years settings needs to have someone to be named as being specifically responsible for safety.

Areas of responsibility

Once appointed, the person responsible for safety should look at the physical environment and the routines in place for maintaining a safe environment. The named worker has responsibility for:

- arranging inspections of the premises on a regular basis;
- making an inspection after an incident or change in use/purpose has happened;
- maintaining accident records and organising practice drills for evacuation and fire;
- maintaining first aid provision;
- providing information to parents of existing safety plans;
- taking a leadership role in developing, implementing and monitoring safety plans;
- regularly reviewing the accident records of the facility to identify areas for improvement;
- arranging and supervising work that needs doing;

- providing to officials inspecting the premises the safety plan, timeframe for its implementation and any other documentation required.

Once appointed the person responsible for safety should look at the physical environment and the routines in place for maintaining a safe environment.

The early years environment

The building

If the building has more than one purpose and has to be shared with others then there should be an agreed safety plan for the shared areas. Check that all shared areas comply with your own safety plan before allowing children to access them. Consider the following questions:

- Does the building have to be shared with other organisations?
- How much storage space is there and does it have to be shared?
- What access do children have to different parts of the premises?

Safety routines

Safety should be included as part of everyday practices without being seen as something that is extra to the daily routine. It should become second nature for staff to consider the environment in which they work and identify hazards to either themselves, their colleagues or children.

Routine tasks

Assessing, monitoring and maintaining safety

Not everything needs to be checked every day but it is important to draw up a checklist that can be signed and dated to make sure nothing is forgotten. The safety plan should identify what needs to be checked on a daily, weekly, monthly or yearly basis. Future dates for inspections should be put in the diary to remind staff when they are to take place, and an independent inspection of the early years setting of premises, equipment and policies should be undertaken. Such safety checks include:

- a visual inspection by walking around the premises making sure that safety equipment is in good order and being used;
- checking safety gates are in place and in good working order;
- ensuring storerooms are closed and not accessible to children or visitors;
- ensuring floors are clear of clutter and spillages, and are clean and well maintained;
- checking that all equipment works by physically testing it.

Buying, installing and using equipment

Early years settings should have written guidelines for the purchasing, installing and use of new equipment. Such guidelines should state that only equipment that complies with current safety laws and standards is purchased. Once purchased, information about their use and cleaning protocols should be made available for staff.

Access to the early years settings

There should be clear procedures for managing access not only to make sure that children stay on the premises but also to prevent unwanted visitors gaining access.

Access can be controlled by a number of things including:

- the height of handles on doors and locks on windows;
- use of security systems of alarms, door keypads, intercoms, name badges, CCTV;
- promoting staff awareness of other people on the premises of visitors, contractors or other users;
- information to staff, parents and visitors through posters, notices and leaflets.

Security measures

Security measures can include:

- a system for reporting suspicious incidents;
- staff reporting strangers on the premises;
- security lighting at entrances, footpaths and building facades;
- surveillance system such as CCTV or security patrols;
- use of intruder alarms;
- automated fire detection system;
- marking of property and secure storage of expensive equipment;
- secured area for waste and recycling bins.

Provisions for managing access include:

- having a book that visitors are required to sign on entering the premises, stating the purpose of the visit with arrival and departure times;
- setting up procedures for staff, children, parents and visitors that use identity checks;
- establishing what to do if children are not collected at the agreed time;
- requesting written permission from parents if children are to be picked up by another adult.

Record keeping

It is very important that accurate and concurrent records are kept whether they are paper based or on computer. It is essential that there are:

- up-to-date contact details for each child, including home phone number, work contact details and where parents or carers are usually based while the child is at your facility;

- accurate details of any medication, medical or physical conditions or allergies that a child may have;
- details of each child's General Practitioner and surgery contact details;
- daily register of attendance;
- an accurate record of all accidents that happen to children or staff members, in a special accident record book;
- records of those visiting the premises.

All records should be available for inspection and reviewed on a regular basis. They are a legal record and important for insurance purposes and provide valuable information. As such they can help with forming policies and when undertaking health and safety audits of the premises. If reviewed regularly the records can identify areas of practice that need to be improved. Any changes that are made must be recorded in the accident record book to demonstrate the steps that have been taken to prevent similar accidents happening in the future.

Communication

Staff training

The safety plan should form the basis of standard training for all early years staff. All staff should be kept informed and up-to-date with any changes to the safety plan. Through regular inspections, training programmes and agenda items at team meetings staff can have a clear understanding of how to create a culture of safety.

Teaching parents and families

The parents and families of children should be included in all your safety messages so that they can understand the reasoning behind what has been put in place:

- keep parents aware of safety practices and their role in helping to maintain these practices;
- make the safety plan available;
- explain the behaviour expected and why;
- gain permission from parents and families to take their child to hospital in case of an emergency;
- demonstrate the use of any safety equipment you may have;
- actively involve parents and families in any first aid courses you run and provide them with accident prevention leaflets.

Teaching children about safety

It is the responsibility of staff to ensure that the environment in which children are cared for does not include exposure to unnecessary risks and hazards. Whilst it is necessary for them to learn about taking risks children between the ages of three and five years old have a limited idea of danger. What can be done is to teach them by:

- setting a good example in everyday activities;
- showing how to use play equipment properly;
- explaining about potential risks and hazards;
- reinforcing safety messages and good behaviour.

Planning for safety

Drawing up a safety plan

You should have a written safety plan to give to parents and carers. This will also provide a reference point for auditing and future development. There are three main parts to a safety plan:

- the aim;
- the current situation;
- future plans.

A safety plan should start with a general statement of safety saying what you hope to achieve. The current situation should be described in terms of the:

- facilities;
- staff and their different roles and responsibilities;
- equipment available and the standard procedures to be followed for when it is used.

Action plan

An action plan should be included in the safety plan, with a timetable stating when the future improvements will be made. This will include identifying any gaps in current practices and procedures and how they can be improved. Any list created should be prioritised according to the urgency of the work, the finances available, and restrictions to the facility and the mix of staff if it involves staff training.

Consulting with staff and parents about improvements and how they can be achieved is useful as they often suggest ideas and initiatives that one person on their own might not.

Finally the safety plan should always be reviewed on a regular basis annually and after any incident has occurred.

General information

[give an introduction to your early years setting, who you are and the type of services provided]

Person responsible for safety

[include the name of the member of staff responsible for safety and who to contact when that person is not available]

Outline plan of the area

[provide a simple drawing of the early years setting covering both the inside and outside areas]

Emergency first aid procedures

[include the name of the member of staff who is responsible for first aid, which may be the same person responsible for overall safety. Also include information about where first aid kits are kept and the procedures that will be followed if an accident happens]

Buying and using equipment

[list the criteria followed when purchasing equipment and the protocol for supervising children when they use such equipment, e.g. climbing frame]

Rules for acceptable behaviour by children, families and staff

[state the accepted behaviour and the action that will be taken should it not be followed; this could be linked to your complaints procedure]

Checklists for maintenance procedures

[state what your policy is on maintenance of equipment and the procedures in place to achieve this]

Outside trips and outings

[provide information on the procedures in place when children leave your early years setting]

Education and training programme on safety

[state the type and frequency of education and training provided to staff and how their knowledge is updated, including fire drills, safety talks and general inspections. You may also wish to link this to teaching children about safety by being good role models in everyday activities and using play equipment properly]

Figure 1.1 Suggested safety plan

Legal requirements

- Have a safety plan.
- Appoint a named safety worker.
- Have secure systems in place for managing access to the premises.
- Know what to do if children are not collected by their parents or named carer.
- Keep accurate records of accidents, inspections and maintenance.

Best practice checklist

- Have an independent annual inspection of the premises.
- Have guidelines for the purchase and use of new equipment.
- Provide induction training and annual updates for staff.

Self review activity

Look at the suggested safety outline plan and consider the following:

- Compare it to your own current safety plan:
  - Does your plan cover similar or different topics; if the latter how does it differ and why?
  - Have you got rules for behaviour of staff, children, parents and visitors to the premises and how were they decided?
  - What is your policy for access to the premises?
  - What do you do if someone other that the child's parent or named carer comes to collect them, or if no one turns up at the agreed time?
- If you have not got a safety plan use the suggested outline and draw up your own safety plan.
- Consider the training programme provided for staff and how it can be improved.

Summary

This chapter has considered the importance of drawing up a safety plan for early years settings and appointing a safety officer to make sure that the premises comply with the welfare requirements that focus on ensuring that appropriate safety measures are taken to avoid dangerous situations. This includes assessing security of the premises and making sure that children stay safe on and off the premises.

2 Developing a safety culture in your setting

Introduction

This chapter looks at the requirements necessary for implementing a health and safety policy in the workplace. Not only the premises but also the equipment used within it need to be maintained in a good state of repair to ensure they do not become a hazard to children, staff and visitors. A health and safety policy affects all activities within the early years setting. It must be used to ensure that hazards have been identified and risks assessed to protect those on the premises. Involving staff in its development and implementation encourages a positive health and safety culture.

Key requirements for implementing health and safety

Key elements of a health and safety policy

A health and safety policy is a document specific to your setting that states how you manage health and safety. It is unique to the individual premises and provides information on who does what, when and how they do it.

If more than five people are employed then you must by law have a written statement of the health and safety policy. This should be written and revised by those working on the premises, as managers and staff all have experiences that are worthwhile to the development of such a policy. The policy should be reviewed and revised on a regular basis, e.g. annually, and also after any emergency situation or if there have been operational or organisation changes.

An alternative to writing your own policy is to use the services of a private health and safety consultant, but it is extremely important that the policy is specific to the premises and involves all the staff.

Most organisations set out their policy in three sections:

- a statement of intent which sets out the commitment to managing health and safety effectively and what needs to be achieved;
- an organisation section that states who is responsible for what;
- an arrangements section that contains details of how you are going to achieve the aims of the policy.

There may be sections of a health and safety policy that you require help with. Involvement of employees and safety representatives in identifying problems and seeking solutions can be one way to achieve this. Health and safety covers a wide range of issues, some of which you are competent to assess for yourself, but there may be specific issues where a greater level of knowledge and expertise is needed. Table 2.1 provides some questions to consider if outside expertise and knowledge are needed.

Table 2.1 Checklist for identifying the need for outside help

Question	Yes	No
Do you have evidence of exposure to something that might cause harm?		
Are you unsure whether you have identified *all* the hazards involved in your work?		
Are you uncertain if any hazards are a risk to staff, children or visitors?		
Are you unsure whether you have done everything necessary to control the risk?		
Are you thinking about introducing new working practices, equipment or processes that might impact on staff health and safety?		
Are rates of sickness and absence a problem?		
Do you think you should analyse the proportion of sicknesses and absences that might be work related?		
Have you noticed a pattern of ill health or accidents you can't explain?		
Have staff reported symptoms of ill health that they think are work related?		
Are you aware of reports of health and safety problems in other early years settings?		
Have you had any 'near miss' incidents?		
Have you had any compensation claims?		
Have you any member of staff who is returning to work who has particular health and safety needs?		
Are you unsure about what the health and safety law requires you to do?		

If you answered yes to any of the questions you should consider the following points:

- Have you analysed the problem as fully as possible?
- Do you think you need help?
- Have you asked your staff and their representatives?
- Is there anyone in the early years setting who can help you?
- Do they need extra or refresher training before they can help?
- Have you compared your practices against other early years settings or what is considered to be best practice?

The following health and safety specialists may be of help:

- health and safety managers
- environmental health officers
- engineers
- occupational hygienists
- occupational health professionals
- ergonomists
- radiation protection advisors
- non-ionising radiation advisors
- physiotherapists
- microbiologists
- health protection advisors.

Should help be needed it is worthwhile preparing a written specification covering the following points:

- the problem and why you cannot manage it yourself;
- information about the early years setting;
- what you want the specialist to do;
- what you would consider to be a successful outcome;
- the resources you can offer and a named contact point to support the advisor;
- when you want the work to be completed;
- how and when you want reports;
- any other relevant information.

Advice before you write a health and safety policy

The health and safety policy is a plan that sets out how you are going to manage health and safety. It states your commitment to health and safety and informs staff of their responsibilities and the steps that they need to take to meet their duties.

Before writing the policy it is important to understand the legal duties and appoint a competent person to manage health and safety on your behalf, depending upon the size of the premises. There is a legal duty to undertake a risk assessment to identify any aspects of the premises that could cause harm to:

- children
- staff

- members of the public
- the environment.

The outcome of the risk assessment will then form part of the arrangements section of your policy.

What to put in a health and safety policy (Figure 2.1)

The *Health and Safety at Work etc. Act 1974* states that you have to put your policy in writing and then put it into practice.

The statement of intent

The statement of intent is the general aims with regard to the health and safety of staff and should be signed and dated by the most senior person employed by the premises. There is no set format as to what to include in the statement, but it is often only a single page long. Most statements of a safety policy will include:

- the commitment to ensure the safety of staff, children, parents, visitors and contractors who enter the early years setting and of anyone else to whom there is a responsibility;
- who is ultimately responsible for health and safety in the early years setting;
- which staff have special responsibilities for aspects of health and safety, giving their names;
- that all staff are responsible for taking care of their own health and safety and that of the people they work with;
- that you recognise the legal duties of the early years setting and that you will provide a safe working environment, equipment and methods of work;
- the organisation and arrangements in place to support the policy.

Some of the ways in which the policy statement can be brought to the attention of the staff are by:

- including it in the staff handbook;
- providing a copy at induction;
- including a copy with the contract of employment;
- posting it on the organisation's intranet site;
- posting it on notice boards;
- making the duties in the policy part of the staff members' workplace objectives.

The organisation

Responsibility for health and safety rests with the employer, although many duties can be delegated to managers. If duties are delegated then individuals should be competent and have received training to demonstrate that they have the skills and knowledge required. The statement should show clearly how duties are allocated with key job titles named and their roles and responsibilities defined.

You can identify:

- who will do the risk assessments;
- who will do the workplace inspections;
- who will ensure the safety of specific tasks or work activities or areas of the early years setting.

This section may include a diagram or flow chart showing the management structure and the responsibilities of the:

- manager
- supervisors or team leaders
- staff.

The duties of the competent person you have designated should be mentioned in this section along with their contact details.

The arrangements

In the arrangements section you should describe the systems and procedures for making sure staff health and safety in the workplace is maintained. All of the hazards should be addressed, including procedures for carrying out risk assessments and dealing with fire and arrangements for providing training and first aid.

This section is very important and should be user-friendly which can be achieved by listing any hazards alphabetically, by individual rooms or specific areas.

A **hazard** *is anything in the early years setting that could cause harm either to people or to the environment. A* **risk** *is the chance, however large or small, that the hazard could cause harm.*

The risk assessment will have highlighted areas that pose a risk and the measures that are currently in place to reduce the risk happening. The additional arrangements that have been identified to control or minimise the risks further should be set out in the arrangements section of the policy and may include:

- training of staff;
- using signs or notices to highlight specific risks;
- improved safety equipment such as personal protective equipment of gloves, aprons, facial protection;
- replacing hazardous chemicals with environmentally friendly alternatives;
- improved lighting or fitting anti-slip flooring.

Attention should be focused on the greatest risks to individuals or those risks that could affect the most people.

Health and Safety Policy Statement
Health and Safety at Work etc. Act 1974

This is the Health and Safety Policy Statement of [insert name of early years setting]

Our statement of general policy is to:
[insert aims of the early years setting on health and safety]

Signature: [name of employer] _____

Date:_____

Review date:_____

Responsibilities

Overall and final responsibility for health and safety [insert employer's name]

Day-to-day responsibility is delegated to [insert name if applicable]

The following staff have responsibility in the following areas [insert name and area/topic of responsibility]

All staff have to co-operate on health and safety matters and not interfere with anything provided to safeguard their health and safety. They must at all times take reasonable care of their own health and safety and report any concerns to an appropriate person as agreed in this policy statement.

Health and safety risks arising from work activities

Risk assessments are carried out by [insert name]

Findings of risk assessments are reported to [insert name]

Actions to be taken to remove and/or control risks are approved by [insert name of person responsible]

[insert name] will be responsible for making sure that any action is implemented and that they have removed and/or reduced the risks identified

Risk assessments are reviewed every [insert time frame] or when activities change, whichever is earliest

Consultation with staff

Staff representative is [insert name of person responsible]

Safe equipment

[insert name] is responsible for identifying all equipment requiring maintenance

Figure 2.1 Template of a health and safety policy (HSE 2011)

[insert name] is responsible for making sure effective maintenance procedures are drawn up

[insert name] is responsible for making sure that all identified maintenance is implemented

Any problems found should be reported to [insert name of person responsible]

[insert name] will check that any new equipment meets health and safety standards before purchase

Safe handling and use of substances

[insert name] is responsible for identifying all substances that need a COSHH (Control of Substances Hazardous to Health) assessment

[insert name] is responsible for doing the COSHH assessments

[insert name] is responsible for making sure that all actions identified are implemented

[insert name] is responsible for making sure that all relevant staff are told about the COSHH assessments

[insert name] will check that new substances can be used safely before they are purchased

Risk assessments are reviewed every [insert time frame] or when activities change, whichever is the earliest

Information, instruction and supervision

The Health and Safety Law Poster is displayed at [insert location] and leaflets are available from [insert name of person responsible]

Health and safety advice is available from [insert name of person responsible]

Supervision of young workers/trainees will be the responsibility of [insert name of person responsible]

[insert name] is responsible for making sure that staff working at locations under the control of other employers are given relevant health and safety information

Competency for tasks and training

Induction training is provided for all staff by [insert name of person responsible]

Job-specific training is provided by [insert name of person responsible]

Figure 2.1 (continued)

Jobs needing special training are [insert job roles]

Training records are kept [insert location and name of person responsible]

Training is identified, arranged and monitored by [insert name of person responsible]

Accidents, first aid and work-related ill health
Health surveillance is required for staff undertaking the following jobs [insert job roles]

Health surveillance is arranged by [insert name]

Health surveillance records are kept by [insert name]

First aid boxes are kept [insert location]

The appointed persons/first-aiders are [insert names]

All accidents and incidents of work related illness are recorded in the accident book, which is kept by [insert name of person responsible and where it is kept]

[insert name] is responsible for reporting accidents, diseases and dangerous occurrences under RIDDOR to the enforcing authority

Emergency procedures, fire, flood, bomb scare and evacuation
[insert name] is responsible for making sure the fire risk assessment is carried out and implemented

Escape routes are checked by [insert name of person responsible and when it is done]

Alarms are tested by [insert name of person responsible and when it is done]

Emergency evacuation will be tested every [insert frequency]

Monitoring
To check the working conditions and make sure that safe working practices are being followed, we will [insert your procedures, e.g. spot-check visits, investigating any accidents of ill health]

Risk assessment
[insert your risk assessment]

Figure 2.1 (continued)

Risk assessment

The important things to decide when undertaking a risk assessment are whether the hazard is serious and whether there are precautions in place to keep the risk of injury small. A good example of this is electricity; it is dangerous and can kill but the risk of this happening in the early years setting with modern construction regulations is low provided that the building conforms to these regulations and electrical equipment used such as kettles or heaters does not have bare wires or worn flexes.

Looking for hazards

A walk around the premises should be the starting point when identifying hazards. Those undertaking the risk assessment should ignore trivial issues and concentrate on any hazards that could result in causing serious harm to an individual or that might affect several people, for example:

- poorly maintained floors or stairs that people could slip or trip on;
- materials or chemicals that are a fire risk;
- exposed moving parts of equipment;
- hot surfaces e.g. exposed radiators, or food trolleys;
- parked vehicles that block fire exits or are a hazard to children and parents;
- poor wiring of electrical appliances and fittings;
- build up of dust and dirt;
- lack of guidelines for moving and handling procedures;
- noise;
- poor lighting;
- extremes of temperature.

In addition:

- ask staff if they can think of any other hazards that might not be immediately obvious;
- look at manufacturer's instructions on equipment.

Identifying people at risk

It is not necessary to list individuals by name but they can be grouped together by the work they undertake or by their use of the building:

- cleaners, contractors, maintenance workers, administrative staff;
- those who may be vulnerable to certain risks and need particular attention such as
  - children
  - visitors
  - students
  - inexperienced staff
  - staff working in isolation
  - expectant workers;
- members of the general public, especially if there are fund-raising events.

Evaluating risk

Evaluate the risks and decide whether the existing precautions are adequate or whether more can be done. It is important to think about how likely it is that each hazard could cause harm, which will help to identify whether more needs to be done to reduce the risk occurring. Even after all precautions have been taken, there will always be some risks that remain. It is necessary that the remaining identified significant hazards are categorised as to whether they are high, medium or low risk.

It is important that the following questions are asked:

- Have you met the standards set by legal requirements?
- Does what you have done represent good practice?
- Have you reduced the risk as far as is reasonably practicable?

It is important to remember that the main aim is to reduce all risks as much as possible.

Drawing up an action list

If things need to be done, an 'action list' should be drawn up and any risks identified as being a high risk and/or those that could affect the most people should be prioritised.

When taking action consider:

- Have you provided adequate information, instruction or training?
- Are the systems/procedures already in place adequate?
- Is it possible to get rid of the hazard totally? If not, how can the risks be controlled so that harm is unlikely?

The principles of controlling risk should be applied in the following order:

1. try a less risky option
2. prevent access to the hazard
3. organise work to reduce exposure to the hazard
4. use personal protective equipment
5. provide an area where washing or first aid can be undertaken.

Recording the findings

If five or more people are employed there must be written records of the significant findings of your assessment, and staff must be informed of the findings.

A risk assessment checklist should show that:

- a proper check was made;
- those who might be affected were asked about the risk;
- all obvious significant hazards were included;
- the precautions taken are reasonable and the remaining risk is low.

Written records are useful for future reference and can help if an inspector asks what precautions have been taken, or if you become involved in any civil liability action. They also act as a reminder to monitor any particular hazard or precautions taken. Written records should be kept for a minimum of three years.

When writing the report it is acceptable to refer to material that is already published on health and safety procedures, which includes:

- guidance from the Health and Safety Executive;
- manufacturer's instructions;
- your own safety procedures;
- your arrangements for fire safety;
- your general arrangements and policies.

Reviewing the assessment

As a living document the risk assessment must be reviewed when anything changes or is introduced into the early years premises that could lead to a risk of new hazards. These include new equipment, new buildings or temporary structures, or change of substances and procedures. It is not necessary to amend the assessment for every new change, but it is necessary that there is an annual review to check that the precautions for each hazard are still adequate to control the risk. If the precautions are not adequate, it is necessary to identify the action needed to be taken and record the outcome of that action.

Developing a safety culture

Safety means freedom from danger or hazards and is the result of individual efforts to achieve this. The attitude of staff and employers to health and safety can have an impact. Poor attitudes, such as the following, can lead to danger:

- cynicism
- fatalism
- showing off
- laziness
- recklessness
- overconfidence
- forgetfulness
- ignorance
- carelessness.

Good safety attitudes help ensure workplace safety. Good health is a safety plus, as fatigue is a frequent factor in accidents.

Legal requirements

● Compliance with health and safety legislation.
● Keep written records of accidents, including those that are reportable under the *Reporting of Injuries, Diseases and Dangerous Occurrence Regulations 1995* (RIDDOR).

Best practice checklist

● Have a written health and safety policy.
● Provide training on health and safety for new members of staff and update their knowledge annually.
● Make sure there are arrangements for monitoring and reviewing the policy.
● Know what to do if there is any health and safety emergency.
● Think fire safety – have regular testing of alarms and evacuation procedures.

Self review activity

The five steps to assessing risk in the workplace are:

1. look for the hazards
2. decide who might be harmed and how
3. evaluate the risks and decide whether the existing precautions are adequate or whether more can be done
4. record your findings
5. review the assessment and revise it if necessary.

Read again the section on risk assessment and then, using the five steps to assessing risk, walk around your early years setting, identify any hazards and discuss these with your colleagues to see if they agree with you.

Summary

Health and safety encompasses a wide range of topics but they all require you to promote a culture of safety and compliance with the current legislation within your setting. Undertaking a risk assessment provides information about the setting that can be used to establish an action plan. This can in turn be prioritised, implemented, measured, reviewed and then used to periodically audit the system overall.

3 The essentials of health and safety legislation

Introduction

By providing the right environment and taking appropriate precautions it is possible to prevent people being harmed or becoming ill through their work. Complying with health and safety legislation is not expensive, time consuming or complicated; it is about encouraging everyone to become safety conscious and creating a safety culture. To achieve this problems have to be recognised, assessed, agreed and acted upon. This chapter provides an introduction to the current regulations that form the basis of health and safety within the UK.

The essentials of health and safety in early years settings

Health and safety is about preventing people from being harmed at work or becoming ill by taking the right precautions and providing a safe environment. Duties under the legislation apply to both employers and employees in early years settings, including those who, like contractors, come onto the premises to do repairs and maintenance.

Responsibilities for health and safety in early years settings are based on the *Health and Safety at Work etc. Act 1974* and its associated regulations. As far as is reasonably practicable, the health and safety of staff, children, parents and visitors while on the premises or out on organised outings must be protected. Risk assessments and audits must be carried out as part of measures taken to minimise or control risks. Everyone has their own roles and responsibilities.

Responsibilities of the employer

Overall responsibility for health and safety remains with the employer, who provides as far as is reasonably practicable for the:

- health, safety and welfare of staff;
- health and safety of children in the early years setting and on off-site visits;
- health and safety of visitors to the early years setting and of volunteers involved in any activity.

The employer must also:

- have a health and safety policy and arrangements to implement it;
- assess the risks of all activities and introduce ways to manage these risks and inform employees of what to do.

Whilst it is possible to delegate safety tasks to individuals, the ultimate responsibility always stays with the employer.

Responsibilities of the employees

Staff also have responsibilities under health and safety law and must:

- take reasonable care of their own and others' health and safety;
- co-operate with their employers;
- carry out the activities in a safe manner in accordance with any training and instruction they have received;
- inform their employer of any serious risks that they have identified.

Assessment of risk

All activities that are performed on the premises must be assessed for their level of risk. Once this has been done, the employer must decide how that level of risk can be reduced or eliminated.

Employers' liability insurance is compulsory. If the local authority (LA) is not the employer, the certificate should be clearly displayed on the premises. While public liability insurance and professional liability insurances are not compulsory they are often considered to be essential in practice.

You should also display the Health and Safety Law Poster on the premises; this can be obtained from HSE Books (ISBN 9780717663149).

Welfare requirements of the Early Years Foundation Stage (EYFS)

Since September 2008 early years settings have been inspected by the Office for Standards in Education, Children's Services and Skills (Ofsted) under the *Childcare Act 2006* (DFE 2006) using the *Statutory Framework for the Early Years Foundation Stage* booklet (DCSF 2008). The aim of the welfare requirements is to support early years settings to make sure that their premises provide a secure and safe environment in which children can learn and develop their potential.

Both the general and specific legal requirements of the welfare requirements must be complied with by all early years settings and Ofsted may give notice to the provider if they consider that they have failed to comply with any of the welfare requirements. This includes information about how the early years setting has not complied with the welfare requirements, what they can do to comply and the time frame in which any action must be completed. It is important to note that it is an offence for an early years setting not to comply with any Ofsted notice under the welfare requirements of the EYFS.

Meeting the welfare requirements

The welfare requirements are in three sections: general legal requirements, specific legal requirements, and statutory guidance. Early years settings must comply with all the legal requirements and should take into consideration the statutory guidance. Where the requirements state that Ofsted must be notified of an event or a change, this must be in writing wherever possible in advance of the event happening. If advance notice isn't possible then Ofsted must be informed as soon as possible but *not* later than 14 days after the event taking place.

Group providers are expected to have written copies of all policies and procedures and should make sure that all staff have copies of these policies and procedures as part of their induction. Parents should also have the policies explained to them and all parents must have access to the policies.

Schools are not required to have separate policies for EYFS if their own policies cover the requirements.

Early years settings must conduct a formal risk assessment of the environment and activities that children are exposed to. These must be constantly reassessed and any necessary adjustments made to secure the children's safety at all times.

The general welfare requirements

Safeguarding and promoting children's welfare

The early years setting must:

- take steps to safeguard and promote the welfare of children;
- promote the good health of children, prevent the spread of infection, and take appropriate action when they are ill;
- manage children's behaviour effectively and appropriately for their stage of development and individual needs.

Suitable people

The early years setting must make sure that:

- adults looking after children, or with unsupervised access to children, are suitable;
- adults looking after children have the appropriate qualifications, training, skills and knowledge;
- staffing arrangements are organised to make sure that children are safe and have their needs met.

Suitable premises, environment and equipment

The early years setting must make sure that:

- the outdoor and indoor spaces, furniture, equipment and toys are safe and suitable for their purpose.

Organisation

The early years setting must make sure that:

- they plan and have systems in place so that every child receives an enjoyable and challenging learning and development experience specific to their individual needs.

Documentation

The early years setting must:

- maintain records, policies and procedures required for the safe and efficient management of the setting which meet the needs of the children.

The specific legal requirements

Safeguarding

The early years setting must have an effective policy in place to include:

- roles and responsibilities of individual practitioners and managers;
- name of the lead practitioner and their role and responsibilities;
- what to do when concern has been raised about a child's welfare or safety including documentation;
- what to do when informing local statutory children's services, agencies, Social Services or the police of concerns about a child;
- what to do when there has been an allegation against a member of staff or volunteer;
- the information to share with parents about safeguarding children procedures before their child joins the setting;
- how parents will be informed about concerns and actions taken under specific circumstances;
- the management of confidentiality and information sharing;
- the requirements of initial and on going training for staff about safeguarding children.

Information and complaints

Early years settings must provide the following information for parents:

- daily routines;
- types of activities undertaken by children;
- staffing levels;
- provision of food and drinks for children;
- all policies and procedures;
- complaints procedure;
- how to contact Ofsted if parents wish to make a complaint;
- what to do if a parent fails to collect a child at the appointed time;
- what to do if a child goes missing.

The following information must be gained from parents before a child is admitted to the early years setting:

- emergency contact numbers;
- special dietary requirements, preferences or food allergies;
- special health requirements;
- who has legal contact with the child and who has parental responsibility;
- written parental permission to seek emergency medical advice or treatment.

Other requirements include:

- procedure for managing concerns and complaints from parents;
- written record of complaints and their outcomes;
- investigation of all complaints about welfare requirements within 28 days of receiving the complaint;
- provide Ofsted, on request, a written record of all complaints made during any specified period and the action taken as a result of each complaint;
- give parents free access to developmental records about their child.

Premises and security

Early years settings must make sure that:

- both the indoors and outdoors premises are safe and secure;
- children are only released into the care of people named by their parent;
- children do not leave the premises unsupervised;
- steps are taken to prevent intruders entering the premises.

Outings

Early years settings must make sure that:

- children are kept safe whilst on outings;
- a risk assessment is carried out before each outing including the required adult to child ratios.

Equality of opportunities

Early years settings must:

- have an effective policy on equal opportunities;
- have a policy to support children with learning difficulties and disabilities;
- if getting government funding have regard for the Special Educational Needs (SEN) Code of Practice.

Medicines

Early years settings must:

- have a policy for administering medicines including how to support individual children with medical needs;
- keep written records and inform their parents of all medicines given to children;
- have written permission from parents for any medicine before giving it to a child.

Illnesses and injuries

Early years settings must:

- have at least one person with a current paediatric first aid certificate on the premises at all times when children are present;
- have at least one person on outings who has a current paediatric first aid certificate;
- have first aid training approved by the local authority and consistent with the guidance in the *Practice Guidance for the Early Years Foundation Stage* (2008);
- have a first aid box with appropriate contents for children;
- keep a record of accidents and first aid treatment;
- inform parents of any accidents or injuries to their child and any first aid treatment given;
- discuss with parents the procedure for children who are ill or have an infection and may be infectious to others;
- inform Ofsted of the action taken if there is any serious accident, illness or injury to or death of any child whilst in their care. Notification must be as soon as possible and within 14 days of the incident happening. It is an offence if an early years setting fails to do so without a reasonable excuse.

Food and drink

Early years settings must:

- have fresh drinking water available at all times;
- make sure that all meals, snacks and drinks when supplied are healthy, balanced and nutritious;
- make sure that those preparing and handling food are competent and comply with food hygiene regulations (*The Food Safety Act 1990 (Amendment) Regulations 2004*);
- inform Ofsted of any incidents of food poisoning that affect two or more children on the premises. Notification must be as soon as possible and within 14 days of the incident happening. It is an offence if an early years setting fails to do so without a reasonable excuse.

Smoking

Early years settings must provide a smoke-free environment for children.

Behaviour management

Early years settings must:

- not threaten corporal punishment or use or threaten any form of punishment that could have an adverse impact on the child's well-being;
- not give corporal punishment to a child on their premises, and as far as is reasonably practicable, ensure that corporal punishment is not given to a child by:
  - anyone who cares for or who is in regular contact with children
  - anyone who lives or works on the premises;
- have an effective behaviour management policy in place that is followed by all staff members.

Suitable people

Safe recruitment
Early years settings must:

- make sure that there are systems in place to assess that those who have regular contact with children are suitable for employment;
- obtain an enhanced Criminal Records Bureau (CRB) Disclosure for every person over 16 years of age who:
  - works directly with children;
  - lives on the premises where childcare is provided;
  - works on the premises where childcare is provided (except if they work there when children are not present, or if they work in another part of the building where children are not present);
- not allow staff unsupervised contact with children if their suitability hasn't been checked;
- keep records of the information used to assess individuals' suitability to prove to Ofsted that checks have been made;
- meet any requirements of the Independent Safeguarding Authority (ISA) scheme.

All registered early years settings must notify Ofsted of:

- any change in the address of the premises;
- any proposal to change the hours when childcare is provided that includes the provision of overnight care;
- any significant event that will affect the suitability of the early years setting or anyone who cares for, or is in regular contact with, children on the premises.

All early years childminders must notify Ofsted of:

- any change in their name or address;
- any change of people 16 years or older living or working on the premises (this excludes people who don't work when children are present or if their work is in a part of the premises where children are not present).

All early years settings other than childminders must notify Ofsted of:

- any change to the person managing the setting;
- any change in the name or registered number of the company managing the setting;
- any change in the name or registration number of the charity managing the setting;
- any change to the 'nominated individual' where childcare is provided by a partnership, body corporate or unincorporated association;
- any change to the individuals who are partners or members of a childcare's governing body where it is provided by a partnership, body corporate or unincorporated association where the sole or main purpose is providing childcare.

The *Childcare (Disqualification) Regulations 2009* (DCSF 2009) state that registered settings must inform Ofsted of any court order or reason for disqualification from registration applicable to themselves or any other person living or working in their household.

Alcohol/other substances

Early years settings must ensure that anyone working directly with children must not be under the influence of alcohol or any other substance that might affect their ability to care for children.

Qualifications, training, skills and knowledge

- Childminders must have within six months of registration attended a training course and hold a current paediatric first aid certificate.
- All supervisors and managers working in other early years settings must make sure that all staff are trained to the appropriate level of qualification.

Staffing arrangements

- Registered group settings must have a named deputy who can take charge when the manager is absent.
- Early years settings must meet the requirements for adult to child ratios as stated in the *Statutory Framework for the Early Years Foundation Stage* (2008).
- The required ratios still apply for childminders providing overnight care.
- In other early years settings providing overnight care, required ratios apply and at least one member of staff *must* be awake at all times.

Suitable premises, environment and equipment

Risk assessment

All early years settings must:

- carry out a risk assessment and review it regularly, at least once a year or more frequently if required;
- using the risk assessment process identify areas of the environment that need to be checked regularly;
- maintain records of when and by whom the risk assessment was carried out;
- decide how frequently risk assessments need to be reviewed and reassessed;

- take all reasonable steps to reduce to a minimum any hazards both indoors and outdoors to children.

Premises

Registered early years settings must:

- inform Ofsted of any change to the premises that may affect the amount of space available and the quality of childcare available. Notification must be as soon as possible and within 14 days of the change taking place. It is an offence if a provider fails to do so without a reasonable excuse;
- take reasonable steps in case of fire to ensure the safety of the children, staff and others on the premises, and have a clearly defined procedure for the emergency evacuation of the premises;
- have appropriate fire detection and control equipment which must be in working order (e.g. fire alarms, smoke detectors, fire extinguishers, fire blankets).

Outdoor and indoor spaces

Registered early years settings must meet the following space requirements:

- 3.5 m^2 per child for children under two years;
- 2.5 m^2 per child for children two years old;
- 2.3 m^2 per child for children aged three to five years;
- that as far as is reasonably possible facilities, equipment and access to premises are suitable for children with disabilities;
- that the premises whilst open are just for the use of childcare;
- that there is public liability insurance in place.

Organisation

Early years settings must:

- have effective systems in place to meet the needs of the children;
- assign a key person to each child;
- promote equality of opportunity and anti-discriminatory practice for each child;
- have a balance of adult-led and child-initiated activities of indoor and outdoor play;
- undertake observational assessment to plan children's individual needs;
- plan and provide experiences appropriate to each individual child's stage of development.

Documentation

Early years settings must record the following data for each child in their care:

- full name;
- date of birth;
- name and address of each parent and carer known to the provider;
- who the child normally lives with;
- emergency contact details of parents and carers.

As part of the Early Years Census settings must record and submit the following information to their local authority of children receiving free entitlement to early years provision:

- full name;
- date of birth;
- address;
- gender;
- ethnicity;
- special educational needs status;
- the number of funded hours taken up during the census week;
- total number of hours (funded and unfunded) at the setting during the census week.

Early years settings must keep the following information and documentation:

- name, home address and telephone number of the setting and anyone else living or employed on the premises;
- name, home address and telephone number of anyone else who has regular unsupervised contact with children attending the early years setting;
- daily record of the names of the children looked after on the premises, hours of attendance and the names of their key workers;
- certificate of registration, to be displayed and shown to parents on request;
- record of the risk assessment clearly stating when it was carried out, by whom, date of review and action taken following a review or incident.

Ofsted inspections

Ofsted is the independent, non-ministerial government department that is responsible for inspecting and regulating early years provision and registered childcare. The organisation's full title changed in 2007 to the Office for Standards in Education, Children's Services and Skills but it is still known as Ofsted.

Inspections are aimed at evaluating the provision of the early years setting using the EYFS. There are no exemptions under the welfare regulations of the EYFS as they are concerned with fundamental issues of child safety.

A sample of policies and procedures will be checked at an inspection including arrangements for safeguarding at every inspection.

Ofsted may visit at other times:

- to check on actions given at an inspection;
- to consider a change of conditions of your registration if requested by yourself;
- when something about your registration has changed, such as an extension to the premises;
- if a parent or other person complains about an early years setting.

Health and safety legislation applicable to all places of work

Whilst the overarching legislation is the *Health and Safety at Work etc. Act 1974*, there are a number of other regulations that require you to take action in response to certain hazards.

Management of Health and Safety at Work Regulations 1999

These regulations generally make more explicit the requirements for employers to manage health and safety under the Act and apply to every work activity. Employers are required to carry out risk assessments, make arrangements to implement necessary measures, appoint competent people and arrange for appropriate information and training to staff.

Workplace (Health, Safety and Welfare) Regulations 1992

These regulations cover a wide range of basic health, safety and welfare issues including ventilation, heating, lighting, workstations, seating and welfare facilities. The regulations require that workplaces are suitable for everybody including those with disabilities. Areas such as doors, passageways, stairs, showers, sinks, toilets and workstations should be accessible to the disabled.

Health measures require the workplace to be well ventilated and the temperature to be warm enough to achieve 'thermal comfort' (usually between 13 degrees centigrade and 16 degrees centigrade). The lighting of the workplace should help people to work and move about safely and should not itself create a hazard. Places should be clean and waste removed and stored in suitable containers. Information is also given about the workstations and seating requirements for employees that is appropriate to the tasks undertaken; any seats should support the lower back and footrests should be provided for those who cannot put their feet flat on the ground.

Safety measures include the need for maintenance of equipment, devices and systems. It covers traffic routes for pedestrians and vehicles, keeping them separate from each other. Walkways for pedestrians should be free of obstructions, not slippery or uneven, to prevent trips, slips and falls. On stairs handrails should be provided at least on one side of every staircase with no open sides to the staircase. There should be no opportunity for anyone on the premises to have access to dangerous substances in tanks, pits or anything that someone could fall into. Whilst it should be possible to open windows they shouldn't be a risk to anyone when open. Any doors and gates should be appropriately made and fitted with safety devices if necessary.

Finally, welfare measures require that toilet and washing facilities are accessible, clean, have hot and cold water with soap and clean towels and that there are separate facilities for men and women with a lockable door for use by one person at a time.

There should be an adequate supply of drinking water along with suitable facilities for rest and breaks where employees regularly eat meals at work. And there should be suitably secure facilities to store workers' own clothing and any special clothing.

Personal Protective Equipment at Work Regulations 1992

This requires employers to provide appropriate protective clothing and equipment for their staff. Personal Protective Equipment (PPE) covers a wide range of items including protective clothing for carers such as disposable aprons, gloves, and eye and facial protection as necessary.

Provision and Use of Work Equipment Regulations 1998

This requires that equipment provided for use at work is safe for the purpose intended. It should be maintained and staff provided with information and training on its use.

Manual Handling Operations Regulations 1992 (Amended 2002)

The regulations apply to a wide range of activities that cover the moving of objects by hand or bodily force. As far as is reasonably possible staff should avoid any manual handling that will result in risk of injury. Assessment of tasks should be made to include the ability of the individual, the load and the task. Such assessments apply to both inanimate objects, such as boxes and equipment, and animate objects which can be people or animals.

Health and Safety (First Aid) Regulations 1981

These regulations apply to all places of work and to the self-employed. They require the employer to provide adequate and appropriate equipment, facilities and personnel to allow first aid to be given to staff if they are injured or become ill at work. Records should be kept of any injuries or accidents and comply with the *Data Protection Act 1998*. Recommendations are made as to what constitutes a first aid box and what training and qualifications are needed to become a first-aider.

Health and Safety Information for Employees Regulations 1989

Employers are required to display a poster telling staff that they need to know about health and safety.

Employers' Liability (Compulsory Insurance) Act 1969

Employers are required to take out insurance against accidents and ill health to their staff so that they have a minimum level of cover should someone make a claim against them for compensation.

The Reporting of Injuries, Diseases and Dangerous Occurrences Regulations (RIDDOR) 1995

Employers are required to notify certain occupational injuries, diseases and dangerous events to the Health and Safety Executive. Incidents should be recorded in an accident book and include:

- death of a person;
- major injury where someone is taken to hospital or needs immediate medical attention;
- over-three-day injuries where someone is off work for a period of time related to an accident or injury at work;
- specific diseases.

Electricity at Work Regulations 1989

This requires that people in control of electrical systems make sure they are safe to use and maintained in a safe condition. The regulations are intended to control the risks around the use of electricity at work.

Fire Precautions (Workplace) Regulations 1997

These regulations require employers to undertake a fire risk assessment of the workplace, looking at preventing fire and controlling and escaping fire safely.

The Management of Health and Safety at Work and Fire Precautions (Workplace) (Amendment) Regulations 2003

These regulations allow employees to claim damages in a civil action, if they become ill or have an injury because their employers breach the *Management of Health and Safety at Work Regulations 1999* and the *Fire Precautions (Workplace) Regulations 1997*. Employers can also bring actions against employees who breach their duties under the 1999 Regulations.

Regulatory Reform (Fire Safety) Order 2005

Fire safety law changed in October 2006 with the introduction of this safety order. It abolishes the need for business premises to have a fire certificate and the law now places emphasis on reducing risk and preventing fires. The Fire Safety Order requires a 'responsible person' (usually the employer) to carry out a fire risk assessment and put in place fire safety precautions to minimise the risk to life and to keep the assessment up to date.

Control of Substances Hazardous to Health (COSHH) Regulations 2002

The law requires employers to assess the risks from hazardous substances and take appropriate precautions to control exposure to hazardous substances to prevent ill health.

Health and Safety (Display Screen Equipment) Regulations 1992 (Amended 2002)

Employers are required to protect the health of staff by reducing the risks from working with VDU screens.

The Food Safety Act 1990 (Amendment) Regulations 2004

The *Food Safety Act* and amended regulations are the basis of domestic food law and apply to all of Great Britain. Food hygiene laws affect all food businesses including catering, farming, manufacturers, distributors and retailers. Since 2006 the Food Hygiene Regulations for the four countries of the United Kingdom cover hygiene requirements throughout the food chain (farm to fork) and general food safety:

- *The Food Hygiene (England) Regulations 2006*
- *The Food Hygiene (Scotland) Regulations 2006*
- *The Food Hygiene (Wales) Regulations 2006*
- *The Food Hygiene (Northern Ireland) Regulations 2006.*

Advice about food hygiene and legislation can be obtained from local Environmental Health Officers based at the local Environmental Health Department.

Legal requirements

- Undertake a formal risk assessment process of the environment and children's activities.
- Have written copies of any policies and procedures required by the welfare requirements.
- Make sure you have employer liability compulsory insurance and display the certificate.
- Take preventive measures to reduce the risk of spreading infections in children and take appropriate action when they become ill.
- Report all work-related accidents, diseases and dangerous occurrences.
- Clearly display the Health and Safety Law Poster.
- Employ staff with the suitable qualifications, training, skills and knowledge.
- All furniture, equipment and toys for both indoor and outdoor spaces must be safe and suitable for their purpose.

Best practice checklist

- Be aware of the hazards and risks involved where you work.
- Write down your health and safety policy.
- Include health and safety on induction for new staff and have regular annual updates.
- Take advice from an expert if you are unsure about any aspect of health and safety.
- Encourage safety awareness and safety practices in everyone.
- Consult staff on health and safety matters.

Self review activity

Develop an induction programme to introduce new staff in your early years setting to the subject of health and safety.
    You might:

- look at the key issues on health and safety and consider the regulations as they relate to your own premises;
- consider what are poor safety attitudes and how these can be turned into good safety attitudes;
- emphasise particular topics such as security, fire safety, first aid or moving and handling as they relate to working with young children;
- create a quiz to cover the key points covered in the session;
- undertake an assessment of your setting with new staff to get them to identify hazards and assess risks.

Summary

Those working in early years settings have a legal duty to provide children with a safe environment by working to high safety standards. This chapter has presented an introduction to the current legislation and regulations and how they relate to the EYFS welfare regulations.

4 Safety inside the early years setting

Introduction

Unlike the outdoors, which is often considered to be a dangerous place, indoors is thought of as being safe and secure. However, children under five years old commonly experience accidents indoors. The implications for the early years setting mean that the hazards children need to be protected against must be identified and actions taken to keep them to a minimum. This chapter looks at the types of accidents that can happen and the hazardous areas that can be found inside the early years setting, and discusses the ways that hazards are identified and risks reduced.

Types of accidents

For children over the age of one year accidental injury is the biggest single cause of death in the UK, and in 2002, 320 children under the age of 15 years died because of an injury or poisoning (Child Accident Prevention Trust 2003). The majority of these accidents are due to falls by children either slipping or tripping on the same level, such as on a pavement or rug. Babies and young children are also sometimes hurt after falling from one level to another, such as from a chair, bed or changing table onto the floor or on or from the stairs.

In children, scalds happen more often than burns and are mostly due to hot drinks. House fires cause the most accidental deaths of children, with 32 children dying in 2002.

While the majority of suspected poisoning cases in children needed little or no further treatment, in 2002, over 26,000 children under five years were taken to hospital after a suspected poisoning.

Common types of accidents

Trips and falls

Children slip and lose their grip or their balance when playing and are hurt not only by falling off the play equipment, but also by hitting themselves on the equipment as they fall. Colliding with other children and hitting fixed or moving equipment are also common causes of injury. Over 75 per cent of accidents that happen to children in play areas are due to falls. Less common types of accidents include:

- cuts and crush injuries when a child comes into contact with protrusions, pinch points and sharp edges on equipment;
- strangulation when children's clothing, especially scarves, drawstrings or cords, catches on equipment;
- entrapment injuries when the head or shoulders become stuck.

It is important to remember that even very young babies, while they might not be mobile, can wriggle, kick or roll into situations that could become hazardous such as rolling off a work surface or changing table. Once babies start crawling they can start to climb onto furniture and windowsills.

If furniture is not stable there is always the risk of injury from it tipping over or moving if it has wheels. Anchoring heavy items of furniture to the wall, moving beds and chairs to remove access to windows to prevent children climbing up and falling, and fitting window locks or safety catches that stop the window opening more than 6.5 cm all help to reduce the risk of injuries.

Finally, to reduce the risk of injuries on the stairs, fit safety gates at the top and bottom of the stairs.

Cuts and abrasions

With the increased use of glass in modern buildings there is also an increased risk of cuts to young children. Glass is a major hazard and comes in a number of forms including ordinary glass, laminated safety glass and toughened safety glass. Any glass that is fitted must comply with British Standard BS 6206 and if in doubt seek expert advice from a Glass and Glazing Federation glazier.

Having access to sharp knives, scissors, razors and gardening tools can also be a cause of cuts. Safe practice can be achieved by:

- having safety glass fitted in doors and windows;
- marking large areas of glass with stickers to let people know it is there;
- fitting safety catches on drawers that contain sharp cutlery and knives;
- keeping kitchen gadgets, sewing materials and gardening tools out of reach of young children;
- replacing glass in bookcases with safety glass;
- checking outdoor areas for broken glass, rusty nails and used drink cans etc. before children are allowed to play;
- wrapping any glass carefully in newspaper before placing it into the bin.

Abrasions can be caused from falling and scraping knees or elbows, and whilst thought of as minor injuries, they do hurt and can become infected. The designated first-aider should be available to deal with the situation by cleaning any wound and contacting NHS Direct or the practice nurse at the local health centre or GP surgery if further advice is needed.

Burns and scalds

Around 95 per cent of all thermal injuries happen to children in the home. Such burns and scalds result in over 100,000 people every year attending hospital with their injuries, which range from minor to fatal and are due to a wide variety of causes. Just under half of these injuries happen to children under the age of five years old (Department of Trade and Industry 1999).

Hot drinks are the most common single cause of scalds in children, with babies and toddlers particularly at risk from pouring cups and mugs of tea and coffee over themselves. Steam or boiling water from kettles and hot oil or fat can cause scalding and young children can also be scalded by hot water from the tap.

The burns injuries that children suffer from happen after contact with open fires, cookers, barbeques, fireworks, matches, cigarette lighters and candles.

The following actions can prevent injuries:

- fitting smoke alarms and checking that they work on a regular basis;
- not holding or picking up a child with a hot drink in your hand;
- keeping mugs away from the edges of tables and work surfaces, out of sight and reach of young children;
- using kettles that have short or coiled flex that are out of sight and reach of young children;
- making sure young children don't play with hot taps;
- ensuring all hot water is delivered below 46 degrees centigrade to avoid scalding;
- always running cold water into baths and sinks before adding the hot;
- always checking the temperature of food or drink when heated in a microwave before giving it to a child;
- remembering that barbeques remain hot for several hours after they have been used;
- fitting fireguards to all heaters and fires including radiators;
- not letting children play with candles or leaving them burning unattended;
- keeping matches and cigarette lighters out of sight and reach of young children.

Suffocation

Asphyxia, when the body is deprived of oxygen, caused by suffocation can be due to pillows, baby bedding of duvets and uncovered plastic mattresses, plastic bags and wrappings and pets overlaying a baby.

Babies are at increased risk of suffocation if they sleep in adult beds as experts state that under eight months of age a baby is unable to roll away or crawl if they become trapped under a quilt, blanket or pillow or trapped between the bed and the wall. Falling asleep with a baby on the sofa also increases the risk of the child being suffocated and is not advised.

Prevention of such accidents includes:

- not using pillows, duvets, quilts and bean bags for children under one year old;
- never using strings, ribbons or ties on very young children's clothing;
- keeping plastic bags and clingfilms from children;
- not sleeping with a baby in your bed or on the sofa as they can be accidentally suffocated;
- placing babies on their back to sleep, making sure they don't get trapped in the covers.

Choking

Choking occurs when there is a blockage caused by a foreign body preventing the passage of air to the lungs. Blockages can be at the back of the throat, or further down in the trachea or bronchi of the lungs. Sometimes a foreign body is swallowed and gets stuck in the oesophagus causing similar symptoms to that of choking. The most common cause of choking accidents is food.

To prevent choking accidents follow safe eating tips:

- don't leave babies alone with a feeding bottle or food;
- closely supervise children at mealtimes;
- teach children to remain seated during mealtimes;
- cut food into small pieces that cannot become lodged in the airways;
- teach children not to talk or laugh when they have a mouthful of food;
- teach children to chew their food slowly and thoroughly and to put only as much food into their mouths as they can chew comfortably.

Other causes of choking include:

- coins, marbles, watch batteries;
- household items, pen caps, plastic bottle caps, buttons;
- toys and inflated balloons.

Poisoning

Many children under the age of five are admitted to hospital every year because of un-intentional poisoning. In the UK 26,000 children went to hospital because of poisoning during 2002, with six children dying, one under the age of five years old (CAPT 2004a).

Most hospital admissions are due to swallowing medicines, with analgesics being the most common, but other medicines include tranquillisers, anti-depressants, vitamins and sleeping tablets. Other substances that children swallow and which can cause harm are:

- household and garden chemicals;
- household products of bleach, disinfectant and dishwasher powder.

These products can cause burns to the mouth, throat, oesophagus and stomach and are highly toxic.

In addition:

- glues, solvents and aerosols can cause burns or sickness if they are inhaled;
- alcohol should be treated as a poison to young children; some mouthwashes contain alcohol;
- cigarettes and tobacco cause sickness if eaten;
- cosmetics can be poisonous to young children;
- perfume, nail varnish remover and hairspray can be harmful if swallowed and many have a high alcohol content;
- essential oils can be poisonous if swallowed;
- plants can have poisonous leaves, seeds or berries, examples being laburnum leaves and seeds, holly berries, lupin seeds and laurel leaves.

Because babies and young children learn about their world by touching and tasting they are likely to put things into their mouths and so are at risk of poisoning. By the time they are 18 months old toddlers can open containers and when they are three they may also be able to open child-resistant tops. Reduce access to poisonous substances and know how to respond to cases of suspected poisoning:

- store household chemicals and medicines away from young children in a locked cupboard;
- store garden and DIY products in a locked outdoor shed or cupboard;
- don't put medicines in the fridge – when labels state 'store in a cool place' it means away from heat and a locked medicine cabinet achieves this;
- keep all medicines and household chemicals in their original containers so that they can be recognised as dangerous substances and the warning labels and instructions followed every time they are used;
- whilst child-resistant bottles are important they are not childproof and work by *slowing down* access to dangerous substances;
- parents and carers should learn basic first aid for babies and young children;
- get advice from a doctor, hospital or NHS Direct if a child has or is suspected of having swallowed something poisonous;
- don't make a child vomit; take the child to the doctor or hospital along with the bottle, packet or item that you think is the cause of the poisoning.

First aid

Accidents can happen at any time, especially for young children, who have a number of bumps, falls and scratches. The majority of these incidents will be minor but some will need professional medical attention and may cause serious injury.

Consideration needs to be given not only to the children who come to the early years setting but also to the staff who work there and any visitors to the premises including parents, siblings and contractors.

The important issue is that those who have an injury or become ill receive immediate attention and that serious cases are identified and the emergency services called where necessary. First aid at work guidelines (HSE 1997) cover the arrangements that must be in place to make sure this happens. It saves lives and prevents minor injuries becoming major ones. The aim of all first aid is to preserve life and to limit injuries. The minimum first aid provision in any workplace is:

- a suitably stocked first aid box;
- an appointed person to be in charge of first aid arrangements.

The welfare requirements of the EYFS specify that there must be in place:

- at least one person with a current paediatric first aid certificate who is on the premises whenever children are present;
- at least one person on outings who has a current paediatric first aid certificate;
- first aid training approved by the local authority that complies with the guidance included in the *Practice Guidance for the Early Years Foundation Stage* (2008);
- a first aid box containing items that are appropriate to the ages of those present on the premises;
- a system that keeps a record of accidents and first aid treatments given.

Preventing accidents

The location and design of a play area can have an impact on child safety.

- The layout must make sure that activities in one area don't interfere with other areas.
- Areas for younger children must be clearly separated from those for older children.
- Paths must be clear of equipment.
- Clear sight lines throughout the play area make it easier to supervise children.
- There should be safe access for children with special needs.
- Lighting must be bright enough to allow for safe supervision.

Minor injuries and near misses

Minor incidents can happen, often with young children frequently falling over and bumping into equipment or people. Injuries such as cuts, grazes and bruises can quickly be dealt with without much disruption, but they are also ideal opportunities to reflect on what might have happened and to be considered as near misses as part of the risk assessment process. It can be a useful learning opportunity to look at what is a minor injury, such as a fall from a climbing frame, and consider the worst-case scenario that could have occurred. Any changes to the play areas can then be made before a serious accident happens.

Moving around safely

Hazardous areas

While a purpose-built facility is the ideal, a number of early years settings are based in converted residential property or linked to other buildings. As such it is important to identify areas in buildings that children should not have access to and which include:

- cellars
- attics
- garages
- roofs
- car parks
- sheds
- balconies
- stairwells.

Alongside such areas you should think carefully about where children regularly go as well as the main rooms. This can include corridors to and from exits or to the toilets, garden or outside area.

Stairs, steps and flooring

The most common area for children, especially those under five years of age, to have accidents is on the stairs, steps and flooring.

- Older buildings are more likely to have uneven steps, open risers and spiral stair-cases.
- Banister spacing should not be wider than 10 cm, or 6.5 cm if babies are cared for, and any horizontal banister spacing should be boarded in as children can easily climb them.
- Babies and young children should always be supervised when on the stairs and safety gates fitted to restrict access to these areas. Safety gates should always be kept closed and children and adults should not be allowed to climb over them.
- The stairs should be checked for wear and tear and immediate repairs made to any loose carpet or treads.
- Consider what is at the bottom of the stairs as it could cause serious injury, e.g. radiators, furniture, glass doors, etc. Radiators may be moved or covered, furniture could be moved and glass doors should be replaced.
- Floors should be kept as clean as possible but not be over-polished so that they cause slips.
- Mats placed on the floor should be fixed to avoid the risk of slips and trips.
- Regularly check floors for wear and tear.
- Make sure floors are even and any changes in height are well defined, e.g. steps, terraces, ramps, etc.

Doors and windows

- Doors should be fitted with safety devices to stop children from trapping their fingers.
- Doorways should be kept clear of furniture and equipment especially if they are emergency or fire exit doors.
- Child-resistant locks should be fitted to windows and any keys should be kept out of reach of children.
- Safety glass must be fitted in doors and low windows.
- Furniture that can be used by children to climb on should not be placed below windows.

Bathrooms and toilets

- All hot taps must be fitted with a thermostatic mixing valve (TMV) to prevent the risk of scalds.
- There should be grab rails and slip-resistant flooring in shower and bath areas.
- Bathrooms and toilets must be able to be unlocked from the outside.

Equipment and furniture

- Any furniture or equipment that is attached to the wall should be secure and stable.
- Children should be discouraged from climbing onto furniture.
- Equipment such as high chairs needs to be fitted with five-point harnesses.
- Check all equipment, furniture, fixtures and fittings on a regular basis for wear and tear and replace when necessary.

- Be aware of sharp corners on furniture and equipment that is at eye level for young children.

Storage areas

- Potentially dangerous equipment such as scissors and craft knives should be stored out of reach of children and kept in drawers or cupboards that are fitted with child-resistant locks.
- Store cupboards should be kept locked and not be accessible to children.
- Store equipment safely in a stable condition so stacked items do not fall onto staff or children.

Kitchens

- Children must not have access to the food and drink preparation area.
- Children should be taught how to use utensils safely.
- Children should be supervised whenever there are hot drinks around.

Specific indoor areas

Space and facility requirements

The *Childcare Act 2006* and the *Statutory Framework for the Early Years Foundation Stage* (2008) for early years settings provide information about the specific space and facility requirements needed when caring for young children. These are that:

- group sizes are never bigger than 26 children, though early years settings can have more than one group;
- premises are clean, well lit, with natural lighting, ventilated and maintained in a good state of repair and decoration;
- there is access to a telephone on the premises;
- rooms are maintained at an appropriate temperature;
- the premises are for the sole use of the early years setting during the hours they are open;
- the indoor play area has the minimum space per child of
  - under two years old – 3.5 square metres
  - two years old – 2.5 square metres
  - three to seven years old – 2.3 square metres;
- a kitchen equipped to give meals and snacks for children and staff on the premises conforms to Environmental Health and Food Safety regulations;
- there is a staff room or area separate from areas used by children;
- there are separate laundry facilities which are not accessible to children.

Toilet and hand washing facilities

- There is a minimum of one toilet and one hand wash basin with hot and cold water for every ten children over two years old.

- Hot water taps should have thermostatic mixing valves fitted.
- There are child-size toilets and hand wash basins as they reduce accidents and promote independence.
- A separate room or partitioned area is available for nappy changing.
- There are separate toilet facilities for adults.
- If toilet doors have locks fitted they should be able to be opened from both sides.

Rest and sleep facilities

- There is a partitioned area or separate room that is warm, well ventilated, with curtains and dimly lit.
- There should be quiet, calm conditions conducive to rest and sleep.
- Cots should be spaced at 18 inches to three feet (45–90 cm) apart to reduce the risk of cross-infection between children (Mathers & Linskey 2009).
- Clean bedding should be supplied for each child.
- Children must always be supervised whether inside or outside when sleeping.

Toys and play equipment

Children under the age of three years are the most likely to have an accident which involves a toy, either when they are playing or by tripping over it, especially when toys are left on stairs or steps. High numbers of accidental injuries are associated with the following toys:

- 5,500 accidents with cars or rocking horses;
- 4,000 accidents with toy boxes;
- 4,000 accidents with model cars, planes and trains;
- 1,500 accidents with soft toys such as teddy bears, dolls and action figures;
- 1,000 accidents with toys that fire objects such as guns, bows and arrows, water pistols or catapults.

(Child Accident Prevention Trust 2004b)

Accidents involving toys can be reduced by choosing the right toy for the age of the child. Most toys have on their packaging a suggested age range reflecting the age groups that the manufacturers believe will find the toy most appealing.

A warning symbol shows that a toy is not suitable for children under 36 months because it may have parts that could choke a young child.

Toys should also conform to the European Standard BS EN 71 which shows that the toy has been tested to agreed safety standards. The Lion Mark is used by members of the British Toy and Hobby Association and shows that a toy has been made to the highest standards of safety and quality.

Finally, there is a legal requirement that all toys that are sold in the European Union carry a CE mark, but this is not a guarantee of quality or safety.

The toy safety code by the Department of Trade and Industry (DTI 1995) advises:

- buy safe toys – cheap toys are not a bargain if a child is injured;
- buy toys that are the right age for the child – read the label and follow the guidelines.

Only give toys that are appropriate to the child's age – young children can choke on small marbles, even balloons;

● throw away broken toys – it is not charity to give broken toys to others for them to have your accident;

● keep toys tidy, and keep stairs and rooms tidy so that children and adults don't fall over toys (Figure 4.1).

Figure 4.1 Storage of toys in play area. (With permission.)

Other ideas for making sure that accidents don't happen with toys include:

● checking that no small parts can become loose and swallowed or inhaled;

● supervising children when they play with beads, buttons and Lego as they might put them in ears or up noses or swallow them;

● storing toys at a safe level, never on high shelves;

● using purpose-built storage boxes with lids that don't trap fingers or close completely trapping a child inside;

● making sure that soft and furry toys only use fillings that are safe, with eyes firmly secured;

● encouraging children to help tidy their toys away to prevent accidents;

● never attaching toys with string around a baby's neck.

Also avoid:

- caps, guns or toys that make loud noises that could damage hearing;
- computer games and videos with flickering lights that may trigger fits in children with epilepsy.

Safety standards for equipment

Hazards can be identified and linked to common everyday items used within the early years setting. The following section identifies some of these hazards and the safety equipment used to reduce such risks.

Other equipment hazards

Changing tables

There are different types of changing tables:

- wooden with guardrails;
- fold-up models;
- hinged chest adapters.

Warning! Hinged chest adapters are not recommended as there have been reports of them toppling over when babies have been placed on them near the outer edge.

When considering what type of changing table to purchase you should:

- check the sturdiness of fold-up models when they are open;
- consider a table with shelves and compartments for storing equipment;
- have a guardrail that is 2 inches (5 cm) high on wooden changing tables.

Dummies, rattles, squeeze toys and teething rings

A risk of choking to babies and toddlers can be associated with these items and other objects that can be put into the mouth. Items with the highest risk are those that have handles or small ends that can be placed in the mouth.

- Do not leave babies or toddlers with any small object in their cot when they are sleeping.
- Do not fasten teething rings, dummies or rattles around a baby's neck.

Toy chests

Accidents have been reported of young children reaching over and into toy chests and the lids falling onto their head or necks. Another potentially fatal, but less frequent, hazard is suffocation when children climb into the toy chest to hide.

If used you should:

- buy toy chests that have detachable lids or doors;
- look for toy chests that have ventilation holes that will not be blocked, or that have a gap between the lid and the sides of the chest;
- make sure the lid does not have a latch.

Hook-on chairs

These are used as substitutes for high chairs and are attached to the edge of the table. There are reports of children falling out of them or of them becoming dislodged from the table. If used, you should:

- not place the chair where the child's feet can push against the table, chair or supports and dislodge it from the table;
- ensure that the restraining straps are used and fastened securely around the child;
- never leave a child unattended when in the chair;
- never use these types of chair on glass top, single pedestal or unstable tables.

Safety equipment

While safety equipment might help prevent a number of accidents, it is no substitute for supervision.

Safety gates

These are designed to prevent access to potentially hazardous areas by toddlers and young children. They are often seen at the top and bottom of stairs but can also be used to keep children in a single room. There are gates that have extensions so that they can fit wider than average corridors and doorways.

Fire guards

These can be fitted to heaters and radiators to reduce the risk of accidental burns for children and adults. They should be suitable for the heater but it is important to make sure that they have no contact with the heater and are at least 20 cm from the heat source, or the guard itself will then become dangerously hot and become a risk.

Smoke alarms

Buildings open to the public should have fire alarms fitted that are tested weekly. The Fire Safety Officer will be able to provide detailed information about what is necessary for the individual early years setting.

Fire blanket

This is standard equipment in the kitchen area and should be fixed to the wall near the cooker. All staff should know how to use it.

Fire extinguishers

These should be checked and serviced regularly and staff should be trained how to use them. The Fire Safety Officer provides information on the most appropriate type of extinguisher for the premises.

Thermostatic mixing valves

These should be fitted to all hot water taps to avoid scalding. It is always best to put cold water into the bath first and then to add the hot. The bath water should be tested before bathing a child whether a thermostatic mixing valve is used or not.

Window locks

These allow windows to be opened wide enough for ventilation but not wide enough for a child to squeeze through. Locks should be appropriate for the type of window and fitted following the instructions.

Cupboard and drawer catches

These are fitted to cupboards and drawers and help to contain potentially dangerous equipment such as scissors and knives. However, some young children are able to open these catches.

Playpens

While not strictly classed as safety equipment, these do serve a function for keeping babies and toddlers in one place. They should be regularly checked as part of a maintenance programme. Slat spaces on a wooden playpen should be no more than 60 mm apart and playpens with a hinge in the centre of the top rails should automatically lock when they are lifted into the normal use position.

Five-point harness

These should be used for babies and toddlers when they are in high chairs or prams but should not be left dangling when not in use as children could get caught up in the straps.

Little Owls Day Care at the Nene School, Wisbech, Cambridgeshire

Challenged with the need to purchase furniture and fittings for the day care centre the staff at the early years setting took into consideration the child-friendly requirements from a health and safety perspective.

Tables and chairs were age appropriate and there were no sharp edges or corners at eye level which could be the cause of injury. Sinks were not only at a height that children could use safely but the taps were press-button and thermostatically controlled to avoid scalding (Figure 4.2).

Figure 4.2 Height-appropriate sink for children to use. (With permission.)

When placing the furniture into different zoned areas, depending upon activities, consideration was given to the flow of traffic so that the children could move between zones without accident or injury (Figure 4.3).

Figure 4.3 Height-appropriate table and chairs for children's use. (With permission.)

Finally, the children can go outside into the garden area as the doors open onto a safe enclosed garden area. Push buttons have been placed above child height on all doors which are exits to the nursery and which lead into the children's centre and the school (Figure 4.4).

Figure 4.4 Doors to outdoor space controlled by child safety push-button system. (With permission.)

Legal requirements

- The premises must be safe and secure.
- A risk assessment must be undertaken and reviewed at least once a year.
- Ofsted must be informed of any change to the premises that affects the amount of space available to children.
- There must be appropriate fire detection and control equipment in working order.
- Premises must be, as far as is reasonably possible, suitable for children with disabilities.
- There must be at least one person who has a current paediatric first aid certificate present on the premises when children are there.

Best practice checklist

- Identify hazardous areas in the premises and also in those areas where children should not be allowed access, e.g. store rooms, kitchens etc.
- Ensure the fixtures and fittings are made safe by having safety glass in doors and low windows.
- Assess the furniture and equipment to make it child-friendly.
- Keep storage areas secure.
- Children should not have access to kitchen and food preparation areas.
- Fit child-size toilets and hand wash basins to promote independence.
- Provide suitable rest and sleep facilities.
- Only use toys that conform to current safety standards and are appropriate for the age of the child.
- Use safety equipment to reduce accidents where appropriate.

Self review activity

Consider the inside of the early years setting. What hazards can you identify and what safety precautions could you suggest to reduce the risk of accidents?

You may consider some or all of the following:

- kitchen and food preparation areas;
- toilet and nappy changing areas;
- corridors and stairs;
- lighting levels in corridors and stairs;
- keeping corridors, doorways and stairs free of equipment;
- cleaning up spillages as soon as possible;
- using safety gates where appropriate;
- using harnesses for babies in high chairs and prams.

Summary

The physical environment inside early years settings can have an impact on safety. Children need to explore and experiment with their surroundings but there should be a balance between this need and a safe environment. This chapter has tried to identify some of the hazards that can be encountered inside early years settings and provide information on safety equipment that may be used to help to reduce such risks. By having systems in place, safety practices can be incorporated into daily routines and potential hazards quickly identified.

5 Safety outside the early years setting

Introduction

Within the curriculum outdoor play is an important part of young children's education. The outside is a natural place for children to be which is enjoyable and fun and where they can be uninhibited and have a sense of freedom (Bilton 2004).

Health and safety has often been the reason given for early years settings not using the outdoor space. This chapter looks at how areas and experiences can be managed safely to ensure that children have an opportunity to discover the outdoors.

Play and activity areas

When designing outdoor play areas there are a number of things to consider to achieve maximum safety. These include simple things like making sure there is enough shade so that children can play out of direct sunlight and that the area can be clearly seen from other areas of the setting to assist with supervision. The play areas should be enclosed with childproof fencing to guard against stray animals entering the area and to prevent the children from wandering out into the local neighbourhood and onto surrounding roads.

Toddler areas

For babies and toddlers there should be a separate play space that allows them to crawl safely with age-appropriate equipment such as climbing frames, slides, swings, ramps, tunnels and wheeled toys. It is essential that this young age group are closely supervised to prevent accidents and injuries.

For babies, if possible there should be an area where prams can be placed so that they can sleep and rest outside where it is sheltered.

Playgrounds

In the UK in 1999 over 150,000 children were injured in school or nursery playgrounds. There is one fatal accident every three to four years (HSE/HELA 2002) on average. These accidents happen in public playgrounds, parks, schools and public houses or restaurants. The play equipment most commonly involved in accidents were:

- climbing frames;
- swings;
- slides.

Other equipment involved in accidents included rope swings, seesaws and roundabouts.

Where to site the play area

Managers of early years settings should think about where the play area is sited and ensure that any equipment is properly designed and installed and maintained. The management systems in place should make sure that the area is maintained in good order and that any damage is repaired quickly. If the play area is already well established, a risk assessment should be carried out and the results used so that an improvement programme can be drawn up, with priorities being identified to cover renewal, refurbishment or removal of equipment; consider installing impact absorbing surfaces (IAS) as part of the assessment process.

Installing or refurbishing play areas

When installing or refurbishing existing play areas it is important to make sure that they meet the requirements of the EN Standards (European Standards – for more details consult the British Standards Institution www.bsi-global.com). A risk assessment should be carried out on the play area that includes both the EN Standards and health and safety legislation.

European Standards

There are two European Standards relevant to safety in children's play areas. BS EN 1176 covers the requirements for design, manufacture and installation of play area equipment. BS EN 1177 states what surfaces should be used in the play area and methods for testing. The standards are not retrospective and are not legally binding but early years settings should know about them and take them into consideration when making decisions about play areas and equipment.

Sawtry Day Nursery, Huntingdon, Cambridgeshire

Refurbishing the outside area into an interesting and safe place for children to explore and learn can be difficult to achieve. At Sawtry there is a large outdoor area which has been zoned into different activity areas.

On exiting the inside space to the outdoors, IAS has been placed and different levels created changing what was a slope into a safe way to transfer between the levels (Figure 5.1).

Playing outdoors can provide a sense of achievement and at Sawtry they have developed areas where children can walk on an all-weather surface that goes around a grass area on which there is a willow tunnel (Figure 5.2).

Around the outer perimeter are signs identifying some of the birds that are being fed next to the bird feeders and ideas of how to link activities with EYFS curriculum (Figure 5.3). There are areas where children can dig (see Figures 5.4 and 5.5) and also a wildlife area of logs where insects and butterflies can be encouraged.

Finally, whilst areas of the grass have to be screened off for reseeding, there is a tree under which the children sit; stories are told and children's drawings are hung from its branches (Figure 5.6).

Figure 5.1 Exit to outside area with safety matting to floor. (With permission.)

Figure 5.2 Willow tunnel for children to explore. (With permission.)

Figure 5.3 Picture and name of a bird next to tree with bird feeder. (With permission.)

Figure 5.4 Digging pit with garden rake and fork. (With permission.)

The signs in the image read:

Digging Pit and Garden Tools

Children learn:

- To describe and talk about what they see
- To Gross and fine motor skills
- To take turns and share
- About the natural environment and living creatures
- To work together
- That tools have to be used safely

Compost Bins

Children learn:

- To recycle materials
- An understanding of decay and changes over time
- To describe and talk about what they see
- Learn about the natural environment

Figure 5.5 Activities linked to learning. (With permission.)

Figure 5.6 Children's pictures hanging from the story tree. (With permission.)

Inspection of play areas

Inspection of play areas must be carried out by a competent person who can be someone who is registered with the Register of Play Inspectors International (RPII) Ltd. Inspectors will be looking for the following to be in place:

● management systems;
● risk assessments;
● action plan and a timescale for action;
● priority for the action areas of concern.

Following the inspection, enforcement action could be considered if there are no management systems, there is an absence of action plans or timescales for action are unreasonably long, and there is no IAS in the impact area.

Different surfaces

Impact absorbing surfaces (IAS) cover a wide range of materials including manufactured tiles, loose particulates and natural materials such as turf, bark and sand.

Installing these surfaces is not the complete answer to preventing injuries in a playground. IAS are tested for their efficacy in reducing the severity of head injuries so they may not be effective in reducing other types of injuries.

Paths, paving and stairs

Any paving and stairs should be made of non-slip materials, with handrails and appropriate protective barriers. Repairs should be made as soon as possible to uneven paving slabs and broken concrete to stop children and staff from tripping or falling over. Paths should also be kept clear of mud and moss-covered paths or patio areas should be cleared as quickly as possible. Chairs and tables should be stacked and stored away and not be accessible to children.

Water

Whether water is held in a garden pond, rainwater butt, paddling pool or a bucket, a young child will go and investigate due to their natural inquisitiveness. Drowning in the garden is the third largest cause of accidental death in the home for the under-fives over the last decade. However, it seems that children are up to 80 per cent more likely to drown in someone else's garden, such as a neighbour's, relative's or friend's.

Due to the dangers, early years settings do not usually have ponds, but if working in an environment where there is one, you should consider the safety advice below.

Children most at risk of drowning

Children need to be closely supervised at all times in and around water with those most at risk being the under-fives, especially one- and two-year-olds, with boys accounting for 78 per cent of incidents in the UK.

The main water features involved are:

- garden ponds;
- swimming and paddling pools;
- other water containers.

Drowning

Children can drown very quickly in very little water (less than 5 cm) so all sources of water can be potentially dangerous, including garden ponds, rivers, lakes, buckets and bowls of water, bath water, puddles and bird baths.

Measures to prevent such accidents include:

- supervising children at all times when they are in or near water;
- never leaving young children alone in the bath;
- not using bath seats as they don't prevent drowning;
- emptying the bath immediately after use;
- draining or securely covering garden ponds;
- not leaving items that can collect rain water in the garden, such as buckets etc.

Pond safety

Ponds are not safe, and are very rarely used in dedicated early years settings. Even the shallowest of ponds, from a child's perspective, can be lethal; a child falling into a 500 mm deep pond is equivalent to an adult falling into 1800 mm of water, the difference being that a child would be unable to climb out of the water. If you do work in a location where a pond is present and cannot be filled in, there is something you can do.

Ponds can be made safer by good design. Ponds should be covered with a grille that should be able to support the weight of a child and be above the surface of the water at all times. Modular interlocking plastic grids that can be made to fit various shapes and sizes of ponds are available, as well as steel mesh. The mesh should be heavy duty (i.e. 6–8 mm diameter wire) and be self-supporting, and have a grid size of no more than 80 x 80 mm to prevent a child becoming trapped. Any method used to secure and lock the frame in place should make sure that there is no risk of children trapping themselves between any moving parts.

Simply fencing off a pond is not good enough. It is only a partial solution and could lead to a false sense of security. Gates can be accidentally left open, and children at three years of age can climb an unsuitable fence within 30 seconds.

Alternatives to ponds

Paddling pools have long been popular but children should never be left unsupervised when they are in use. They should always be emptied after use then turned upside down so that rainwater cannot accumulate.

In summer weather sprinklers are a common alternative; there are now specific child-friendly sprinklers in the shapes of flowers or animals.

Sandpits

Sandpits are a well-liked outdoor activity. They should be placed in partial shade, be well drained and the borders rounded and covered when not in use. Formed plastic sand boxes can be used as they are light enough to remove and replace. Sand used in sand-pits should be specifically purchased for use to ensure it is not contaminated and should be replaced on a regular basis and kept securely covered so that animals cannot use it as a toilet area (Figure 5.7).

Figure 5.7 Sandpit with bucket and spade and counting numbers on the fence. (With permission.)

Having a wildlife garden

Wildlife gardens are increasingly fashionable as a way of introducing children to the natural world by studying it using informal and curricular activities and by practical care of the garden.

Garden plants

Planting sensory gardens is now encouraged in schools and early years settings and helps children to explore the five senses. Many plants, including their fruit and seeds, are safe and good to eat and are recognised as food plants. Most plants found in the home and gardens are ornamental plants or weeds that are not dangerous.

Small children often like to nibble plants and need to be taught not to eat any part of a growing plant. A sensible rule is to make sure that children know not to eat anything that is not recognised as food.

Poisoning by plants in the UK is rare but it is important to have knowledge of any plants that may cause harm to young children. The Royal Horticultural Society (2004) and other horticultural organisations have compiled a list of potentially harmful plants and have developed a Code of Recommended Retail Practice for labelling plants at garden centres and nurseries.

Allergic reaction to plants

As well as the dangers of eating poisonous plants there is the possibility of suffering an irritant or allergic reaction through contact with a plant or its sap.

There are three main types of contact hazards:

- a burning sensation and sometimes blistering of the skin can affect anyone if they have sufficient exposure to irritant sap;
- some individuals who acquire sensitivity to plants that contain chemicals called allergens can suffer an allergic reaction. Often this presents as dermatitis (inflammation of the skin) but in some people it can be a more intense reaction, such as seen in nut allergies;
- a few plants have sap that makes the skin sensitive to strong sunlight. Consequently, contact with this type of plant followed by exposure to strong sunlight causes a very severe localised sunburn with blistering and a long-lasting skin discolouration.

First aid

If you think a child has eaten part of a doubtful plant you should:

- seek medical advice at once from a hospital accident and emergency department;
- take a sample of the plant so that it can be identified;
- not attempt to make the child sick.

In cases of irritant or allergic dermatitis, contact a doctor and take a sample of the plant with you.

Common names of some poisonous plants

Autumn crocus
Bluebell
Calla lily
Cuckoo-pint (lords and ladies)
Daphne
Deadly nightshade
Delphinium
Euphorbia

Foxglove
Hellebores (Christmas rose, Lenten rose)
Iris
Ivy
Laburnum
Lily of the valley
Mandrake
Monkshood
Morning glory
Wisteria.

Ideas for a child-friendly garden

- Grow a herb wheel along with fast-growing salad crops that can be eaten.
- Make a bog garden using an old washing-up bowl.
- Have a bubble fountain or child-friendly sprinkler instead of a pond.
- Make an insect corner with a pile of logs in a shady corner to attract insects.
- Have a planting and growing area using plantpots, tubs, troughs and growbags.
- Have a bird feeding station and put out different types of food to attract a range of birds.

Fences and hedges

Any fencing, whilst useful, can cause concern as young children may try to climb over it. If fences are made of wire they can cut their hands and feet, and hedges can be hazardous to the eyes.

Any gaps in fencing should be less than 100 mm wide, and not have any protruding nails or sharp edges that a child could get stuck on or injure themselves on.

Fences have three main functions:

- they keep children in an area that is safe for playing;
- used with gates they keep animals out of the play area;
- they give children the sense that it is their own area for playing which is separate from their surroundings.

Wherever possible the best materials that can be afforded should be used to reduce the need for frequent repairs and maintenance. Fences should be put up according to BS 1722 and conform to the control recommendations in the EN 1176 (play equipment standard) so that safety hazards are avoided (The Royal Society for the Prevention of Accidents 2004).

There is a wide range of plants that can be chosen to provide a hedge, but some of the plants, such as laurel, can be poisonous. Hedges are often chosen to provide a security screen but some of these plants such as pyrocantha and berberis are very thorny and can cause injuries to adults as well as young children if they try to push through gaps in the hedge. As such it is important to check any hedge for gaps and, for complete safety, chicken wire can be used at the base of the hedge, if it isn't a bush all the way to the ground, to prevent young children crawling through.

Insect bites and stings

Bees, hornets and wasps

These insects have small sacs of venom that are designed to hurt and drive off intruders. They are attracted to bright clothing and strong smelling soaps and perfumes. If they land on adults or children it is important to stand still and not run away or try to hit them, as they will just get agitated. If they do sting, immediately check whether the child has an allergy to stings – usually known as anaphylaxis.

Anaphylaxis *is an extreme allergic reaction that can be life threatening and needs urgent medical treatment.*

Signs and symptoms of anaphylaxis

Every child is different and the signs and symptoms appear almost immediately after being exposed to an allergen and include some or all of the following:

- swelling of the face, throat, tongue and lips;
- a metallic taste or itching in the mouth;
- difficulty in swallowing;
- flushed complexion;
- abdominal cramps and nausea;
- increased pulse rate;
- wheezing or difficulty in breathing;
- collapse or unconsciousness;
- widespread red, blotchy skin eruptions;
- puffiness around the eyes.

Practical guidance

- If a child has an adrenaline pen, and staff are trained and permission given, administer the device.
- If a child collapses or falls unconscious, place them in the recovery position and remain with them until help arrives (all settings should have a trained first-aider who can help and assist with this emergency).
- Call an ambulance immediately if there is any doubt about the severity of the reaction or if the child does not respond to medication.

Keep adrenaline pens readily available to staff and always carry them on trips and visits.

If a child is not known to have an allergic reaction to insect bites and stings it is still important to watch for signs of a reaction. The child can be made more comfortable by checking the site of the sting closely, and if the sting is still in place, gently scraping it out with a credit card or other blunt-edged item. Apply a cold compress to reduce any swelling.

Poisons and chemicals

Other hazards include poisons and chemicals, which should be stored and locked in a secure area with childproof doors as required under the COSHH Regulations (2002). Children's toys should not be stored in the same area or near poisons and chemicals and should be stored well away from all dangerous items that are used outdoors such as power and garden tools. Chemicals should never be poured out of their original containers into soft drinks bottles, as they should always be easily identified to make sure they are handled correctly according to the manufacturer's instructions.

Outdoor play equipment

There is a wide variety of play equipment available for outdoor activities including:

- climbing frames;
- timber structures;
- balancing bars;
- slides;
- seesaws.

For toddlers and babies play equipment can include:

- ramps;
- low slides;
- tunnels.

Trampolines are not suitable for use by toddlers and young children under the age of six years old. Mini-trampettes are a popular alternative, though children must be supervised at all times by an adult when they are used. No more than one child should use them at any one time.

Storage of outdoor equipment

Equipment must always be stored away tidily after use to reduce the risk of anyone slipping or tripping up on it. This includes tables and chairs so that children cannot climb onto them and injure themselves. Garden sheds are tempting places for children to explore and children should never have unsupervised access to them; they should always be kept locked when not in use.

Sun safety

There is an increasing awareness of the dangers as well as the benefits of being exposed to the sun. Infants' skin is sensitive and easily burns because it is thinner and has undeveloped melanin, especially when exposed directly to the sun, the effect of which is increased when it is windy. As a result of excessive heat children can also suffer from heatstroke, which may be accompanied by sunburn. Very young children are not able to control their temperature in the same way as older children and adults, making them more prone to heatstroke. Babies under six months old should be kept out of the sun and after this age children should be kept out of the sun when it is at its strongest. They should be dressed in loose clothing with sunblock applied and wear a hat that covers the back of the neck.

Early exposure to the sun, especially when it is reflected off the sand and sea, can cause skin cancer in later life. All skin types (Asian, African, Caucasian and mixed race) need protection from the sun by using sunscreen and protective clothing. You should have parents' permission to apply sunscreen – otherwise keep children out of the sun. Remember that sunscreen products are only as good as the person who is using them and follow these suggestions:

- stay out of the sun when it is at its strongest. This varies and can be a short period from 11 a.m. to 2 p.m. or anywhere between 10 a.m. and 4 p.m.;
- the face and neck are the areas most affected by skin cancer from too much sunlight. Wearing wide-brimmed hats or hats with a neck protector is advised;
- cover up the body as much as possible by wearing long-sleeved tops and baggy shorts;
- the minimum sun protection factor (SPF) recommended is 15;
- the SPF number refers to how much it enhances an individual's natural sun protection – if you normally burn within 20 minutes, using a sunscreen of SPF 15 would protect you for 300 minutes (20 x 15 = 300);
- most sunscreens work by absorbing ultraviolet rays but some reflect the rays. Ones that protect against both UVA and UVB are the best. Sunscreens should be used to help protect against sunlight, not as a substitute for avoiding exposure;
- some sun tanning lotions do not contain sunscreen and will provide no protection;
- babies under six months old should be shielded from the sun or wear protective clothing if they have to go out in the sun. Sunscreen is not enough;
- you can get sunburnt on cloudy or hazy days;
- when applying sunscreen wait for 20–30 minutes for it to dry and stay on your skin as this is the length of time taken for the chemicals to start working;
- reapply waterproof sunscreen every two hours and after being in the water;
- a lotion of milky gel-type sunscreen is preferable to use with young children rather than clear alcohol-type products;
- remember the slogan of SLIP, SLAP, SLOP. Slip on some clothes, Slap on a hat, Slop on sunscreen.

Heatstroke

We are all susceptible to heatstroke but too much sun can be especially serious for young children as they have difficulty in regulating their own body temperature. Those who suffer from heatstroke will:

- be flushed and feel hot to touch;
- have a fever and rapid pulse;
- be dehydrated;
- be confused and disorientated and have unco-ordinated movements;
- some children may feel sick or be sick.

Serious cases of heatstroke can result in hospitalisation and the individual may fall into a coma and die. If a child is suspected of having heatstroke:

- they must be seen by a doctor;
- keep them in a cool shaded place;
- remove any excessive clothing;
- encourage them to drink cool fluids;
- increase the ventilation by opening the windows or using a fan;
- cool the skin by bathing in cool, not cold, water (15–18 degrees centigrade).

General rules for children

General rules need to be taught to children about health and safety outdoors and certain procedures followed:

- make sure that hats and sunscreen are worn in sunny weather to avoid sunstroke and burning;
- make sure children drink water regularly to avoid dehydration;
- always supervise young children, especially when there is water around;
- teach children to regularly wash their hands, especially after they have handled soil and pets;
- stop children sucking their fingers or biting their nails while outside in the garden;
- clear any cat or dog mess up before children dig in the ground;
- teach the basic rules about handling gardening tools that they can use, and about those that are dangerous;
- keep garden sheds locked using child safety locks;
- teach children not to touch any dangerous chemicals;
- be aware that some plants:
  - can be poisonous, such as berries;
  - can burn the skin or sting, such as stinging nettles;
  - have thorns and hooks, such as roses;
  - have leaves that can cut the skin, such as grasses.

Legal requirements

- Make sure play area surfaces are safe, appropriate and conform to recognised safety standards.
- Look for safe playground equipment that conforms to a recognised safety standard.
- Use impact absorbing surfaces under equipment above 0.6 m in height.

Best practice checklist

- Check children's outerwear does not have hood or neck drawstrings that could cause strangulation if caught in equipment.
- Have separate areas for different age groups so that they use age-appropriate equipment.

- Always supervise children closely to avoid injuries.
- Have a maintenance programme in place and have regular inspections.
- Keep the area free from clutter, litter and debris.
- Create a number of play opportunities such as imaginative play, open play, quiet areas and adventurous play.
- Make sure fences and walls are in good repair.
- Keep all gates closed.
- Have safety rules in place that everyone knows and follows.

Self review activity

Safety can often be seen in negative terms but children need to learn to explore the outside world:

- decide the activities that you would wish young children to experience as part of the early years curriculum outdoors;
- carry out a risk assessment of the outside area and activities to be undertaken and identify any hazards that can be removed or reduced;
- draw up safety rules for children and staff to follow so that the activities you have chosen can be undertaken in a safe manner.

You may consider the following:

- Can the outside area be divided into different zones to facilitate safe play?
- Are equipment and resources stored safely?
- Are children involved in setting up and tidying away?
- Is children's clothing and footwear suitable for the outdoors, whatever the weather?
- Are staffing levels appropriate so that children are closely supervised and supported in all the activities you have provided?
- Have safety practices been discussed with the children so they understand the safety rules?

Summary

Education outdoors is an important part of the early years curriculum and this chapter has discussed the ways in which the outside play area can be made safe for children to use. The use of impact absorbing surfaces and purchasing and upgrading equipment to current safety standards reduces the risk of accidents along with carrying out risk assessment and inspections on a regular basis. Whilst a good design will provide an ideal space to use, it is the level and quality of observation and supervision given to children while they use such space that will ensure they suffer no injury.

6 Preparing for outings and trips

Introduction

Whether an outing is informal, i.e. to local shops and amenities, or is more structured, i.e. to farms or local nature reserves, while providing a valuable learning experience it can also bring an increased risk of accidents. It is possible to reduce such risks by meticulous planning and organisation. This chapter considers the planning needed for successful educational visits outside of the early years setting.

Educational visits

Outings and trips provide opportunities for young children to experience the outdoors in a way not possible in the classroom, and are fun. Careful planning including risk assessment, an exploratory visit to the area, first aid, transport and emergency procedures achieve a successful outing.

Local authorities in some areas set their own levels of supervision for visits while others expect this to be done as part of the risk assessment process. Popular outings and trips include visits to the coast, farms, museums, local parks, the high street, the local wood or nature reserve.

Planning for an educational visit

Guidance for planning educational visits is published by the Department for Education and Skills (1998). When organising an outing or trip you should consider the following points:

- objective of the visit;
- date, venue, length of visit;
- staff to child ratio;
- resources needed;
- estimate of costs;
- appropriate insurance.

Planning should also include:

- contacting the venue to assess its suitability for young children;
- deciding what transport is required;
- deciding who will lead the group;
- undertaking a risk assessment of the trip and an exploratory visit to the venue;
- gaining written parental consent;

- making emergency arrangements;
- making contingency plans for late return.

Adult to child ratio

When planning outings the risk assessment process should include the staff to child ratio requirements which may be more than the specific legal minimum. The following ratios are the minimum legal requirements early years settings must meet:

- one member of staff to every three children under the age of two years;
- one member of staff to every four children aged two years;
- one member of staff to every eight children aged three years and over:
  - this is dependent upon whether the member of staff has a qualified teacher status, early years professional status or other appropriate level 6 qualification as defined by The Children, Young People and Families Workforce Development Council (CWDC).

First aid arrangements

All staff should know about the first aid arrangements and how to contact the emergency services. A fully qualified first-aider with a paediatric first aid certificate must be on the outing. The minimum first aid provision for a visit should be:

- an adequate first aid box;
- appointing someone to be in charge of the first aid arrangements;
- consideration of the number of children in the group and the activity;
- consideration of the type of injuries that might happen and how effective first aid is likely to be;
- establishing the location of the nearest hospital with an emergency department.

Travel first aid box

The minimum contents of a travel first aid box should be:

- a leaflet with general first aid advice;
- six individually wrapped sterile adhesive dressings;
- one large sterile unmedicated wound dressing 18 cm x 18 cm;
- two triangular bandages;
- two safety pins;
- individually wrapped moist cleansing wipes;
- one pair of disposable gloves.

A resusciade (for hygienic mouth-to-mouth resuscitation) is useful to include.

Travel arrangements

- Local authority regulations should be checked in advance of any outing.
- All vehicles must have a current MOT certificate of roadworthiness and be taxed and

insured; if possible obtain photocopies of any documents for your risk assessment.
- All drivers must have a driving licence that covers the type of vehicle they are driving; again, if possible, obtain a photocopy of this for your records.
- All minibuses must have forward-facing seats with seat belts.
- Children under three years old must use a child restraint and not an adult seat belt.
- Child restraints include baby seats, child seats, booster seats and booster cushions (these are manufactured according to different weight ranges).
- EYFS guidelines require that records are kept about the vehicles used, including insurance details and a list of named drivers.

Planning the outing

- Check out where you are going to visit; if the venue has its own risk assessment, ask if they will provide you with a photocopy for your records.
- Identify a person responsible for the trip before you go.
- Obtain parental permissions.
- Tell the children and give them instructions appropriate for their age.
- Make sure that the adult to child ratio is appropriate for the outing.
- Make sure that any equipment or luggage is stored correctly.
- Leave details of the route and the expected time of return with the early years setting.
- Make a list of all who are on the trip and their emergency contact details.
- Have an emergency contingency plan ready that includes getting in touch with parents, evacuation of the vehicle, first aid requirements and what to do if you are going to be returning late.
- If the venue has a fire drill procedure, include this in the instructions to those supervising the outing so that they are aware of fire exits and meeting points on the day.
- Have a list of volunteers going on the outing (this should also include the driver) and a list of named CRB checked staff members attending.

On the day of the outing

- Make sure that the adults and children know who is responsible for whom.
- Make sure that staff members and volunteers know the procedure should an emergency arise.
- Any medication that a child normally has should be taken with them on the trip.
- Have a list of everyone in the group: staff, volunteers and children.
- Make regular checks during the outing that the whole group is present and no-one is missing.
- Ensure all children are easily identifiable (badges or contact bracelets can be used with the name of the early years setting and emergency contact telephone number).
- Avoid identification of children that could put them at risk, e.g. name badges; consider coloured caps or armbands.
- Make sure that children know what to do if they become separated from the group.
- Get children to use a 'buddy' system, so that each child regularly checks that the other is OK. (A variation is the 'circle buddy' system where they form a circle and have a left- and right-side buddy.)
- Make sure that children wear their seat belts when travelling.

- Ensure head counts are carried out when getting on or off transport.
- Keep an eye on the weather.
- Always have an alternative plan in case the itinerary needs to be changed; carry a mobile phone (charged and with sufficient credit) and first aid kit, plus accident book.
- The vehicle should also have its own first aid kit as well as the one from the early years setting.

Local outings

Casual trips to places in the local community near the early years setting can be organised, but as with outings further afield, careful planning makes a successful outing.

Such outings include going to the:

- fire station
- greengrocer's shop
- park
- wood
- canal basin
- museum
- art gallery.

These local outings allow children to explore their own community but any proposed outing should be reviewed for its suitability and whether it is child-friendly and what the learning potentials are for the children.

Whatever the type of visit, whether to a local amenity or further afield to farms or the seaside, the same safety checks need to be undertaken as identified earlier in the chapter.

Farm visits

The highlight of visiting farms for children is to see the animals, especially lambs, kids, calves and foals, and if possible to touch them. All animals carry a number of microbes that can be transmitted to humans and cause infections such as *Escherichia coli* 0157 (VTEC) food poisoning, and more recently *E.coli* 026, which is known by the term 'zoonosis'. Most illnesses are self-limiting and resolve within seven days, but some can cause severe disease requiring hospitalisation. However, simple steps such as hand washing can quickly control the risks from farm visits.

Before visiting the farm

It is always useful to discuss the visiting arrangements with the farm management and check that the facilities available are the same as those described in the Health and Safety Executive (HSE 2000) safety leaflet AIS23.

There are some basic safety rules for children to follow which reduce the risk of infection and include:

- not to kiss any of the animals;
- not to try any of the animal foodstuff;
- washing their hands after any contact with the animals and before eating;
- not to drink from water taps outside of designated public facilities areas;
- not to suck their fingers or put pens, crayons or pencils into their mouth;
- clean or change footwear after the visit and wash hands after doing this.

Pregnant women

Pregnant women should avoid accompanying the group on a farm visit as contact with farm animals at certain times of the year (i.e. contact with lambs in the spring) can result in Listeria infection that has been linked to miscarriage.

Advice to parents

When providing information to parents about a farm visit it should be requested that their children wear appropriate clothing for the weather and for the time of year, and that they bring a change of clothing in case of accidents.

Sturdy outdoor shoes (not sandals) or wellington boots should be worn by children if possible, as farms are working environments.

How to prepare the children for the visit

Before visiting the farm, staff should talk to the children about the day and what rules need to be followed regarding touching the animals, washing their hands and where they will be eating.

During the visit

On the day of the visit adults and children should follow good hygiene practices; it is important to remember:

- children are the responsibility of the early years setting staff throughout the visit;
- children must be supervised throughout the visit, especially when washing their hands to make sure they do it correctly (farm staff may be able to help);
- plenty of time should be allowed before eating and leaving the farm so that the children are not rushed and therefore do not wash their hands;
- if a child becomes ill following a farm visit and has any signs and symptoms such as diarrhoea or vomiting, they should see their doctor and the early years setting should report this to Ofsted within 14 days.

General advice

General advice for farm visits includes the following points:

- wash and dry hands thoroughly after stroking or touching animals;
- do not eat or drink anything whilst walking around the farm, including sweets;

- only eat away from the animals after thoroughly washing your hands;
- do not let children put their face against the animal or kiss the animals;
- keep children's hands out of their mouths after touching animals;
- keep away from slurry and manure and do not touch animal droppings; hands should be washed immediately if they come in contact with them;
- shoes should be cleaned on leaving the farm or when arriving home, and then hands washed thoroughly.

Coastal visits

Outings to the coast can be a popular choice, especially for those early years settings that are near the sea. The risks associated with such outings need to be recognised and linked to other activities that might be considered, such as walking on the beach, paddling in the sea and rock pooling.

In addition to the general rules when organising and planning outings, the following points should be considered:

- obtain advice from the local coastguard, harbour master, lifeguard or tourist information office who will be able to provide information on the local area;
- be aware of warning signs and flags;
- keep away from sewage outlets and areas of beaches that are not for general access;
- know the times of local tides;
- be aware of the dangers of paddling in the sea for young children;
- be aware of the attraction of tunnelling into sand dunes for children, which could then collapse and bury them.

Missing children on outings

As part of the risk assessment process when planning for an outing it is important that this scenario is included and the action to be taken in the circumstances considered.

If, on an outing, it is thought that a child is missing, then immediate action must be taken including the following:

- the person in charge must be informed immediately;
- all remaining children must be accounted for and adequately supervised whilst a search of the local area is undertaken by other staff members;
- if the child is not found in the immediate vicinity then the person in charge must notify the authorities of the venue so that a more thorough search can be undertaken;
- if the child is still not found at this stage then the following people must be informed:
  - the police;
  - other relevant emergency organisations (e.g. RNLI);
  - the early years setting manager;
  - the parent or carer of the child;
  - Ofsted and the Social Services Officer;
- the search will now be organised and led by these organisations.

Informing Ofsted and Social Services is part of the RIDDOR arrangements and an investigation may need to be undertaken.

Legal requirements

- Children must be kept safe on outings.
- Undertake a full risk assessment for each outing, including the required adult to child ratios.
- Review assessments before going on each outing.

Best practice checklist

- Check the place you want to visit before you take the children there.
- Check whether the place you want to go to has suitably qualified staff and what the hazards of the venue are.
- Get consent forms from parents for the visit.
- Tell the children about the outing and give instructions appropriate to their age.
- Make sure you have the correct adult to child ratio following the risk assessment for the visit.
- Make sure that any equipment or luggage taken is stored securely on the vehicle.
- Have a list of emergency contacts for everyone who is going on the outing.
- Have emergency procedures in place, especially for getting in touch with families if you are going to be late returning from the outing.
- Identify who will be responsible for what on the outing before you go.
- Know what the cancellation arrangements will be.
- Check what transport arrangements have been made.
- Provide information to parents, staff and volunteers about the outing.

Self review activity

Plan an outing suitable for a group of three year olds that would contribute to their development and utilise areas of the early years curriculum. Evaluate the plan and its implementation.

You may consider:

- venue;
- time of year;
- staff to child ratio;
- risk assessment;
- health and safety;
- appropriate clothing;
- learning activities;
- children with medical conditions e.g. asthma;
- advice to parents;
- emergency contact details;
- first aid requirements;

- transport;
- parental consent.

Summary

All children must be kept safe on outings while being encouraged to explore their environment. To achieve this the principles of safety awareness are important along with anticipating hazards that might be encountered. This chapter has stressed the need for planning and organisation and the suitability of the location for young children.

7 Aiming for quality and auditing the early years setting

Introduction

Quality is defined as *the standard of how good something is when measured against other similar things*. There is a constant search for excellence and quality, especially when considering the care provided in the early years setting. With the introduction of the Early Years Foundation Stage (EYFS) there is a baseline for comparison between different child-care providers. There are also a number of quality assurance schemes that help early years settings raise the standards of the childcare that is provided. Such schemes are programmes designed to raise standards above and beyond those set by EYFS and show a commitment towards increased knowledge and continuous improvement to practice.

This chapter looks at the issues around quality, audit and standards and how a safety culture can be encouraged.

Quality issues

Quality is very difficult to measure and the meaning of the word varies depending upon your own perspective. Managers, staff and parents all have different priorities in the assessment of quality because of the different roles they have in the early years setting. There is no single, comprehensive indicator of a quality service, though one of the best-known theoretical models is Maxwell's division into six dimensions of effectiveness, efficiency, equity, acceptability, accessibility and appropriateness (Maxwell 1984).

Dimensions of quality: definitions

- Effectiveness – the extent to which objectives are achieved; ideally you should be able to measure outcomes.
- Efficiency – 'value for money'; how to make the most of the resources available.
- Equity – equal treatment or access.
- Acceptability – the manner and environment in which care is provided.
- Accessibility – to include times, location and suitability for those with disabilities.
- Appropriateness – relevant to the needs of the children or priorities of the local authority (LA).

While these definitions may be desirable attributes, they might not be applicable to every situation or environment. Recent attempts to define quality have concentrated on *effectiveness* in that it gives the feeling of achieving a desired goal or of meeting a defined need. However, quality improvement activities often require investment in staff time or resources.

Quality assurance schemes help to raise standards of care and demonstrate commitment to best practice, and to continuously improving practice. Current quality assurance schemes include working in partnership with parents to make sure that individual children's needs are considered and met. They build upon the welfare requirements in the Statutory Framework for the EYFS that are the basis for Ofsted inspections of early years settings. They are also a means by which staff are able to update their knowledge in childcare and show continuous improvement to their practice. Whilst there are a number of quality assurance programmes, such as the National Childminding Association (NCMA) Children Come First quality improvement scheme for childminding networks, since 2007 they are no longer endorsed through the government initiative Investors in Children.

Encouraging a positive health and safety culture

Under health and safety legislation an employer has a legal duty to consult with staff when preparing and completing a safety policy. The benefit of involvement of staff in developing a health and safety policy is a sense of ownership. Along with this, staff may be more likely to comply with the practices because they understand and agree with the reasoning behind their implementation. The person who is actually doing the job is often the best person to advise whether the safe working method will work. This is often referred to as a positive health and safety culture.

The four Cs of a positive health and safety culture are:

- competence
- control
- co-operation
- communication.

Competence involves:

- assessing the skills needed to carry out all tasks safely;
- providing adequate instruction and training for all staff;
- involving all staff in the contribution to the self-reflective evaluation of the setting;
- arranging access to advice and help;
- restructuring or reorganising to ensure the competence of staff taking on new health and safety responsibilities.

Control involves:

- leading by example, demonstrating your commitment and letting everyone know that health and safety is important;
- identifying people responsible for particular health and safety tasks, especially where special expertise is needed;
- ensuring that managers, team leaders and all staff understand their responsibilities and have the time and resources to carry them out;
- ensuring that everyone knows what to do and how they will be held accountable (e.g. by setting objectives).

Co-operation involves:

- chairing your health and safety committee, if you have one, and consulting your staff and their representatives;
- involving staff in planning and reviewing performance, written procedures and problem solving;
- working in partnership with parents to understand and contribute to the policies in the setting;
- working with contractors who come onto your premises.

Communication involves:

- providing information on hazards, risks and preventive measures to staff, contractors and parents;
- discussing health and safety on a regular basis;
- being 'visible' on health and safety.

Monitoring and auditing performance

Setting standards helps to promote a positive culture and to control risks; the standards set out what staff will do to deliver the policy and identify who does what and when and the outcome. Standards must be:

- measurable
- achievable
- realistic.

Standard statements must be measurable. Saying that 'staff must be trained' is difficult to measure if you can't say what is meant by training or who the staff are, in what they should be trained and by whom. If standards already exist, these can be adopted; if not, you will have to develop your own.

Standards that can be measured by audit have three main components:

- structure – the resources and personnel available (quantity and quality)
  - staffing/skill mix
  - equipment required
  - documentation/records;
- process – what you do with the resources to achieve your outcome;
- outcome – the result of the effectiveness of the policy.

One way to make sure that standards are achieved is by borrowing the process of setting SMART/SMARTER objectives from project development. This is a mnemonic used for setting goals to achieve a specific objective. The general accepted terms for the letters are:

S – specific
M – measurable
A – achievable
R – relevant
T – timely
E – extending
R – rewarding

Developing the terms into individual goals and objectives needs an understanding of the terms which are as follows:

Specific:

- Does it specify what you want to achieve?
- Is it a specific behaviour or outcome?
- Can you express the outcomes in a number or percentage?

Measurable:

- Does it include a measure so you can track how well you are doing?
- Is there a reliable system that can help you track behaviours or actions?
- Can you state the objective as a quantity to help with measurement?

Achievable:

- Is the objective achievable and attainable?
- Can you complete what you say within the time available?
- How many factors (beyond your control) could block this objective?

Relevant:

- Is the objective you have set important to the organisation?
- Does the objective focus on positive impact?
- Will the objective set lead to a specific behaviour or outcome?

Timely:

- Do you know by when you need to achieve the objective?
- Is there a start and finish date clearly defined?
- Have you considered competing demands on your time – can you overcome them?

Extending:

- Do you feel that the objective stretches your personal capability?
- Does it contribute to your personal/professional development?
- Does this development have a positive impact on the organisation?

Rewarding:

- Can you express the benefit this objective gives to you?
- Can you express the benefit this objective gives to others?
- Can you express the benefit this objective gives to the organisation?

Using the SMART and SMARTER objectives provides a structure that can be used to successfully achieve the specific legal requirements set out in the welfare requirements of the Statutory Framework for the EYFS.

Ofsted, when undertaking their inspections under Sections 49 and 50 of the *Childcare Act 2006*, has regard to the *Statutory Framework for the Early Years Foundation Stage* document. Ofsted inspectors expect that childcare providers will be able to show how they achieve each of the standards specific to their early years setting. Excepting schools, all early years settings have to be registered by Ofsted when providing for children from birth to the end of the EYFS.

Local authorities are obligated to help those providing childcare delivered by either themselves or others with information, advice and training to meet the requirements of the EYFS. Along with training in EYFS assessment and completion of EYFS profile summaries, for all those childcare providers who Ofsted deems inadequate in the provision of their childcare, local authorities must give information, advice and training to develop their provision within the given timeframe stated by Ofsted.

What audit is and how to do it

Auditing is not a new idea and is practised by a variety of professions to monitor and assess the quality of care that they are providing. The commonest approach to auditing is to set standards against which current practice can be measured and change identified. This is often called 'the audit cycle', and is an ongoing process.

There are four components of the audit cycle which form the process that requires you to:

- reflect on your performance;
- observe your practice;
- compare your practice against that of the current accepted standard (benchmarking);
- implement change.

The purpose of audit is to review current practice by using existing knowledge to improve the service provided. Its intention is to provide feedback to those involved and it is about the application of knowledge. Audit has a dual purpose of improving quality while educating and developing all those involved in the process. It should be seen as a learning process for both the organisation and individuals and needs to be undertaken in an open manner.

Once an audit has been completed, feedback of the results is useful for staff not only to understand the process and outcome achieved but to ensure that everyone is included at all stages. It can be useful to describe the positive elements that came out of the audit along with areas and practices that need improvement. The aim of audit is not about staff appraisal and individuals should not be criticised; it is about improving the quality of service provided. Plenty of time should be given to discussion and to considering the recommendations that fall out of the process.

Finally, once the results of the audit have been discussed, the audit process itself should be reviewed to identify three main areas:

- what went well – look at the achievements; don't start with the negatives because focusing on the positive encourages staff morale;
- what was difficult – identify problems at each stage and how you tackled them; were the standardised checklists useful?
- what are the next steps – if it looks like you can't achieve your standard, what practical steps can you take to do so?

While it might be expected that changes need to be implemented, you may find that it is not always necessary. Audit may show that your standards are being met satisfactorily.

It is important to remember that audit is a dynamic process and is about providing a quality service and constantly improving the level of quality of that service.

Legal requirements

- Maintain records, policies and procedures for the safe and efficient management of the setting.
- Conduct a risk assessment and review it regularly.

Best practice checklist

- Audit should not be judgemental; it looks at what is happening and can lead to informed decision making.
- Good planning makes for a successful audit.
- Setting local standards and criteria is an important part of making audit relevant to your own facility.
- Don't reinvent the wheel, make use of what is already available.
- Audit is a continuous process and is easier the second time around.
- Discuss the findings with all staff as this is a part of the process.
- Undertaking audit helps to improve the quality of care provided.
- Build a portfolio of evidence that shows compliance with welfare requirements.
- A portfolio of evidence includes risk assessments, cleaning schedules, action plans, policies and procedures, minutes of meetings, parent information leaflets etc.

Self review activity

Obtain a copy of the *Statutory Framework for the Early Years Foundation Stage* and read section three 'The welfare requirements'. Look at the welfare requirement for 'Suitable premises, environment and equipment' which states that 'outdoor and indoor spaces, furniture, equipment and toys, must be safe and suitable for their purpose'.

The specific legal requirements ask that a risk assessment is undertaken and reviewed regularly, identifying hazards and keeping these to a minimum. The statutory requirements state that it should cover anything that a child may come into contact with, and that a health and safety policy must be in place.

Once you have read this welfare regulation, review your own setting's risk assessment for the premises and activities that children participate in. Items to consider could include any of the following:

- fire safety;
- security systems;
- water safety;
- boundaries and gates;
- hazardous substances and equipment;
- kitchen and food preparation areas;
- sleeping areas and monitoring arrangements;
- hygiene, cleanliness and reducing the risk of infection;
- reducing the risk of cot death;
- condition of toys and play and sensory equipment;
- floors, stairs, corridors, thoroughfares;
- gas and electricity safety, use of electrical socket covers;
- condition and use of prams, pushchairs, high and low chairs, and safety harnesses;
- meeting space requirements for different age groups.

Summary

This chapter has provided an introduction to the issue of standards, audit and quality. Audit is a structured process that can be used to assess the quality of care given in the early years setting and can be a valuable source of insight as to how something is achieved. Done successfully, it can confirm that everyone is doing a good job and can be a positive reinforcement of best practice.

8 Individual policies and procedures

Introduction

A health and safety policy aims to influence all the activities undertaken in the early years setting, including the people, equipment and materials, and how work is structured. By providing a written policy that encompasses all aspects of health and safety, it shows to staff, parents and outside organisations that hazards have been identified and risks have been assessed, then eliminated or controlled. This chapter provides examples of audit tools to assess the main areas of health and safety, including security, personal safety, fire, first aid, moving and handling, electrical hazards, and hazardous substances.

Security (Table 8.1)

The *Statutory Framework for the Early Years Foundation Stage* (EYFS) welfare requirements state that early years settings have a legal responsibility to make both the inside and outside of the premises safe and secure.

This includes making sure that children are not able to leave the premises unsupervised and that intruders are unable to enter the premises.

The statutory guidance asks early years settings to be aware of and where relevant to consider the following points:

- indoor and outdoor security such as locking of doors, door alarms, security systems, intercoms and name badges;
- awareness by staff of where other people are in the building; information posters and leaflets to remind staff and parents about the need for security and the systems in place to achieve it;
- any additional security measures needed when children stay overnight;
- a system that identifies visitors to the premises recording names, arrival and departure times and the purpose of the visit;
- the arrival and departure procedures for staff, children, parents and visitors to the early years setting;
- the process in place for collection of children by someone other than their parent, preferably where possible getting written permission from the parent.

Security is important as its aim is to protect people and property from fire, theft, accident, loss of power, violent crime etc., 24 hours a day, without interfering with daily life. Security incidents may range from assault, trespass and use of offensive weapons to harassment, threatening or abusive behaviour and criminal acts of theft, burglary and vandalism. For early years settings there is also the concern that children may wander outside the premises through doors or gates that are not secure. Or a child might

Table 8.1 Audit tool for security incidents in the early years setting

Date	Name of early years setting			Name of auditor	
		Yes	No	N/A	Comments
1	There have been issues of trespass in the past 12 months				
2	There have been incidents of vandalism in the past 12 months				
3	There have been cases of theft and/or burglary in the past 12 months				
4	There have been arson attacks in the past 12 months				
5	There has been a local problem of drug or solvent abuse in the past 12 months				
6	There have been attacks/threats on staff and children in the past 12 months				
7	The early years setting is in a low crime rate area				
8	The early years setting is overlooked by busy roads or houses				
9	Boundaries are well defined, preventing intruders entering the premises				
10	There are clear entrances with signs directing visitors				
11	Safe parking is available in a well-lit area				
12	Building is well maintained				
13	The premises are not a multi-building site				
14	There are no areas for intruders to hide unobserved				
15	All doors are secure with locks that are inaccessible to children				
16	Windows and roof-lights are protected against forced entry				
17	There are not many computers, TVs, or DVDs on the premises				
18	There is strong community and parent support				
19	There is a system for reporting suspicious incidents				
20	Waste and recycling bins are locked up every night				
21	There is security lighting of all entrances, footpaths and facades				
22	There is a system of surveillance, e.g. CCTV				
23	There is an intruder detector system on all ground floors				
24	There is a fire detection system				
25	All valuable property is marked and kept in a secure area (use of smart water etc.)				

intentionally be taken by someone other than their parent when they are collected at the end of the day.

As with other aspects of health and safety, it is important to undertake a risk assessment to understand:

- the type and scale of the risk;
- trends or patterns in incidents involving the early years setting;
- security measures needed;
- the efficiency of the chosen security measures;
- how to prioritise, within a realistic timeframe, the additional controls identified in an action plan.

Contacting your local crime prevention officer can be helpful and provide advice about practical measures to take. There should be a system of recording and reporting incidents, even minor ones, so that they can be reviewed and used as a basis for information about the security measures needed.

Fire (Table 8.2)

Welfare requirements of the Statutory Framework for the EYFS include as a legal requirement that early years settings have appropriate detection and control equipment in case of fire and an emergency policy for evacuation of the premises. Statutory guidance also recommends that the fire safety officer inspects sleeping areas and that fire exit signs are in place and fire doors are clear of any obstructions and can be opened easily from the inside.

Whilst it is impossible to be totally immune to fire risk, early years settings can reduce the risk by implementing fire safety management systems. Under the Fire Safety Order (Regulatory Reform (Fire Safety) Order 2005) the 'responsible person' must carry out a fire risk assessment and make sure that everyone on the premises can escape in a safe manner should there be a fire. By everyone it includes not only staff and children but also visitors and external contractors to the premises. The 'responsible person' is often the most obvious person but the regulations state that it should be whoever is in control of the area or systems such as the employer, manager or occupier. They are asked, either on their own or with others, to carry out a five-step risk assessment:

- step one: identify any fire hazards.
- step two: identify the people who would be at risk.
- step three: evaluate the risk of a fire starting, reduce or remove hazards that would cause a fire and provide protection from fires starting.
- step four: record your findings and action taken, prepare an emergency plan, inform relevant people about the plan and provide training.
- step five: review the risk assessment regularly and make changes where necessary.

Fire safety regulations are enforced by the fire authorities who target their resources and inspections at those premises considered to be at the highest risk.

Advice can be obtained from the Fire and Rescue Service and the local fire safety officer. For general fire precautions the minimum standards to be considered include:

Table 8.2 Audit tool for identifying fire hazards

Date	Name of early years setting				Name of auditor	
		Yes	No	N/A	Comments	
1	Staff are trained in evacuation procedures					
2	Fire action notices are displayed					
3	Fire practice drills are held regularly					
4	Combustible materials are identified and stored correctly					
5	Fire doors are regularly inspected and maintained					
6	Fire doors are unlocked and available for immediate use at all times when the building is occupied					
7	Fire doors are identified with fire exit signs					
8	Portable electric or liquid petroleum gas (LPG) heaters are not used (replace naked flame and radiant heaters with fixed convectors or a central heating system)					
9	Tungsten filament bulbs are replaced with fluorescent fittings where there is a risk of combustible materials igniting					
10	Multi-point adapters are not used (additional sockets should be provided where these are used)					
11	Bins holding combustible waste are at least 10 metres away from any building, and are in a secure enclosure					
12	Flammable wall and ceiling finishes have been removed or treated					
13	Display materials are kept to a minimum on escape routes or sprayed with fire retardant					
14	Highly flammable materials are stored in fire-resistant stores away from sources of ignition					
15	Ducts, chimneys and flues are kept clean and in good repair					
16	A 'hot work permit' system is operated and contractors and maintenance staff are provided with fire safety information					
17	A no smoking policy is operated throughout the early years setting					
18	All electrical inspection and testing is kept up-to-date and repairs are carried out promptly					
19	Only a competent nominated person wires plugs, using the correct fuse					
20	Faulty electrical equipment is immediately removed					
21	Flexes are kept as short as possible, equipment with damaged cables is never used					
22	Staff know how to isolate the main electrical supply in an emergency					
23	Fire fighting equipment is placed in correct locations and tested each year					
24	Staff are trained in the use of different fire fighting equipment					

- fire detection and warning system;
- a way to fight the fire:
  - guidance states that the 'rule of thumb' is that you should have one fire extinguisher at least for each floor of the building and for each 200 metres squared (m^2) of floor space;
- ideally, there should be more than one escape route from the building with the travel distance (the distance people need to go before they get out) as short as possible;
- when planning escape routes the time it takes to escape varies depending upon whether the risk of fire starting is high or low. Travel distance is measured from the furthest point in the room to the door, then to a protected stairway to the final exit point of the building. The recommended distances are as follows:
  - for a single escape route travel distance should not be more than 18 metres, 12 metres if the risk of fire is high or 25 metres if the risk is low;
  - if there is more than one escape route travel distance is 45 metres, or 25 metres for high risk and 60 metres for low risk;
- have suitable fire doors that can easily be exited and which don't require keys or specialist knowledge to open;
- other things to consider include:
  - emergency lighting;
  - fire safety signs;
  - training for staff;
  - management systems to make sure that fire safety systems are maintained.

Moving and handling

The *Manual Handling Operations Regulations 1992* (Health and Safety Commission 1992) apply to a wide range of activities, work settings and loads. Manual handling injuries can happen whenever people work and many risk factors are involved. The Health and Safety Commission has prioritised the prevention and control of musculoskeletal injuries (MSI) but not all MSI injuries are preventable. Because of this it is important to encourage staff to report injuries early and access treatment and rehabilitation for those who do get injured. Employers have to consider the risks of manual handling to the health and safety of their staff and consult with them as to how such risks can be reduced.

Employers' responsibilities:

- avoid the need for hazardous manual handling as far as is reasonably possible;
- assess the risk of injury from any hazardous manual handling that cannot be avoided;
- reduce the risk of injury from hazardous manual handling as far as is reasonably possible.

Employees' responsibilities:

- follow appropriate systems of work for their safety;
- make proper use of equipment provided for their safety;
- co-operate with their employer on health and safety matters;
- tell their employer if they identify hazardous handling activities;
- take care to make sure that what they do does not put others at risk.

Assessing the risk

It is important not to create new hazards by changing practices:

- most situations will need simple observation to identify how to make things easier, less risky and less demanding;
- advice from outside experts may be helpful to get started or in difficult and unusual cases;
- records of the main findings of assessments should always be kept if this would be difficult to repeat;
- records do not need to be kept if the assessment is easily repeated because it is simple and obvious, or if the handling operations are low risk;
- generic assessments are acceptable where they are applicable to a number of staff;
- individual risk assessments may need to be carried out for employees with a disability, or those who become ill, are injured or return from a long period of sickness.

In all assessments it is important to identify all significant risks of injury and identify how to make practical improvements. Assessments should not be forgotten or filed away. The purpose of an assessment is to pinpoint the risks associated with the task and to prioritise in which order things should be improved. The assessment should be updated when significant changes are made in the workplace. Once risks have been identified, staff should be informed and the necessary measures taken to avoid or reduce them.

Moving and handling children

Staff need to be able to lift children correctly, both for their own safety and for that of the child:

- stand as close as possible to the child before you lift them and tell them what you are going to do. Keep your back straight and, bending your knees, hold the child firmly around its middle as you lift;
- be sure that there is nothing to hinder the lift, such as loose clothing catching on furniture or forgetting to undo a harness if the child is in a high chair;
- carry the child close to the body, as it reduces the strain on the back;
- only carry one child at a time unless there is a life-threatening emergency situation.

Electrical safety (Table 8.3)

Electricity can kill; poor electrical installations and faulty electrical appliances can also lead to fires that may cause death or injury to others. Approximately 1,000 accidents occur in the workplace and are reported to the Health and Safety Executive (HSE) each year. The 220 voltage of domestic electricity supply can kill or severely injure a child causing burns unless a Residual Current Device (RCD) that cuts out the supply is fitted. All early years settings and homes should have an RCD fitted to protect everyone from incurring an accidental electric shock. Electrical safety should be promoted at all times and careful planning and simple precautions can avoid most accidents.

Table 8.3 Audit tool for electrical safety

Date	Name of early years setting			Name of auditor	
		Yes	No	N/A	Comments
1	Plugs and sockets are placed beyond children's reach wherever possible				
2	Childproof caps and plugs are used				
3	Any plugs and sockets that are warm to the touch are disconnected, marked and reported				Do not use them until they have been repaired or replaced
4	Plugs and sockets fit firmly, needing force to insert and remove them				
5	Plugs are always held when being removed from sockets, never pulled by the flex				
6	All equipment is properly tested and carries an annual test certificate				
7	Only competent electricians make repairs to electrical equipment and wiring				
8	Flexes are checked frequently for fraying, bare wires and other defects				
9	Flexes are kept away from oil, grease or any material that causes deterioration				
10	Flexes are kept out of the way so they do not become tripping hazards or get damaged by people walking on them				
11	Extension leads are rarely used and never overloaded				

The main hazards

The main hazards associated with electricity are:

- contact with live parts causing shock and burns (normal mains voltage 230 volts alternating current (AC) can kill);
- electrical faults leading to fires;
- fire or explosion where electricity is the source of ignition in a potentially flammable or explosive atmosphere.

The risk of injury from electricity is linked to where and how it is used and the risks are greater in wet surroundings, outdoors, and in cramped spaces where there is a lot of earthed metalwork.

Risk assessment

Following a risk assessment, the following suggestions are given as an example of good practice to reduce the risks.

Connections

- Plugs and sockets should be sited beyond children's reach wherever possible.
- Childproof caps and plugs should always be used.
- Plugs and sockets should fit firmly needing some force to insert and remove them.
- Disconnect, mark and report any plugs or sockets that form a connection that is warm to the touch. Do not use them until they have been repaired or replaced.
- Make sure flexes are connected to plugs and appliances correctly.
- Unplug electrical appliances when not in use.
- Always grasp the plug to remove it from the socket – never pull the flex.

Equipment

- All electrical equipment should be properly tested and carry an annual test certificate (portable assessment test (PAT) certificate for portable electrical equipment).
- Only a competent electrician should make repairs on electrical equipment and wiring.
- Use British Electrical Approval Board (BEAB) approved appliances.
- Have an RCD fitted to protect the electric circuit.

Flexes

- Check flexes frequently for fraying, bare wires and other defects. Pay particular attention to the point where the flex attaches to the equipment.
- Keep flexes away from oil, grease or any material that causes deterioration.
- Keep flexes out of the way so that they do not become tripping hazards or get damaged by people walking on them.
- Avoid using extension leads and never overload them. Never use extension leads around children.

Prevention

A system of preventative maintenance should be followed to prevent any injuries. This should include a visual inspection and, where necessary, testing of equipment. Most electrical risks within the early years setting can be controlled by concentrating on a simple, inexpensive system of looking for visible signs of damage or faults. This needs to be backed up by testing as necessary and records of tests and results of inspections should be kept.

Slips, trips and falls (Table 8.4)

Slips and trips in the workplace are the single most common injury at work and make up a third of all reportable injuries and half of the reported injuries by the general public. Undertaking a risk assessment of the environment and getting things right from the start will help to reduce incidents, taking care not to create new hazards when changing practices.

The Health and Safety Executive (HSE) recommends a five-step approach to assessing risks:

- step one: look for hazards that might cause slips, trips and falls inside and outside the premises;
- step two: identify who may be at risk, e.g. staff, children, visitors and contractors;
- step three: consider the risks and identify if there are any precautions being taken to reduce the risks and if they are sufficient;
- step four: document the findings;
- step five: review the assessment regularly and when any alterations or changes are made to the premises.

Some of the risk factors to consider include:

- environmental risks – floors, steps, slopes, changes of levels;
- contamination risks – water, food, litter, spillages;
- organisational risks – tasks being performed, safety culture of the organisation;
- footwear – inappropriate footwear being worn;
- individual factors – amount of supervision, information and training.

Changes to consider include:

- changing where possible to slip-resistant flooring;
- cleaning spillages immediately;
- routine cleaning of floors, choice of cleaning products, allowing floors to dry thoroughly before use, using signs to raise awareness of floor cleaning taking place;
- establishing a 'sensible shoe policy' – flat shoes that enclose the foot with correct type of sole, for staff and children;
- improving lighting to make any hazards more visible;
- providing hand rails and floor markings where there are slopes and changes of levels;
- avoiding trailing cables where people walk or work.

Table 8.4 Audit tool for slips, trips and falls

Date	Name of early years setting			Name of auditor	
		Yes	No	N/A	Comments
1	External steps, paths and parking areas are suitable for the amount of use, have flat, even surfaces and are kept free of mud, leaves and snow				
2	Edges of steps are marked using an anti-slip coating				
3	Lights are replaced, repaired or cleaned before levels of lighting become too low to be safe in outside areas				
4	Playground surfaces are flat and well maintained to avoid collection of surface water				
5	Adequate supervision is provided in playgrounds at all times				
6	Suitable non-slip, water-absorbing mats are provided at entrances				
7	Hidden steps and changes of level at entrances and exits have displayed warning signs				
8	Warning signs are displayed where there is a risk of slipping				
9	Where appropriate, anti-slip coating is applied to areas of smooth flooring in internal stairs and corridors that may become wet				
10	Handrails are provided for internal stairs				
11	Edges of internal stairs are marked with anti-slip coating				
12	Internal lights are replaced, repaired or cleaned before levels of lighting become too low to be safe on stairs and in corridors				
13	Storage racks are provided for children's bags and outdoor wear				
14	Children's practical work is safely displayed				
15	Toys are cleared away and stored safely after use				
16	Staff wear suitable footwear in kitchen and food preparation areas				
17	All spillages are cleaned immediately				
18	Suitable floor surfacing is provided in kitchen and food preparation areas				
19	Warning signs are displayed when cleaning is in progress				
20	All floors are cleaned and dried effectively				
21	All floors are cleaned after children have eaten				
22	There are no trailing cables around the premises				
23	Good housekeeping is maintained				
24	Worn or damaged carpets/tiles are replaced				

Employers have to consider the individual needs of children, staff and visitors who may have disabilities. Things to consider are events such as open days when people who are unfamiliar with the premises are visiting.

Many slip incidents happen in kitchens and food serving areas, so consideration should be given to work surfaces and appropriate flooring. Any catering or cleaning contractors should have an agreement stating how work will be undertaken and the health and safety precautions they will take to reduce the risk of any slip or trip injury happening. The issues to discuss include:

- equipment not to be used;
- the personal protective equipment to be used and who will provide it;
- working procedures;
- number of people to do the work;
- reporting of incidents and keeping records.

Cleaning

There should be detailed information on how staff will manage the cleaning of spillages and the routine cleaning of floors. Wet cleaning can leave a thin layer of cleaning solution on the floor that can take approximately five minutes to dry, resulting in very slippery conditions.

Footwear policy

Footwear is an important part of preventing slip incidents and a 'sensible shoe policy' for everyone can make a significant reduction in slip and trip injuries. This means wearing flat shoes that enclose the whole foot, not sandals or sling-back shoes.

Lighting

Lighting is very important as poor lighting can obscure any hazards, while excessively bright light can cause glare, which also obscures hazards.

Changes to the environment

Where changes or modifications to premises are made, consideration should always be given to reducing and eliminating slip and trip risks in the design stage, such as installing slip-resistant flooring. Adequate facilities have to be provided in buildings for the storage and drying of children's outdoor clothing and for the storage of their other belongings under the *Education (School Premises) Regulations 1999*.

First aid and reporting accidents (Table 8.5)

First aid can save lives and prevent minor injuries from becoming major ones. Under health and safety legislation, employers have to make sure that there are adequate and appropriate equipment, facilities and personnel for providing first aid in the workplace. People at work can fall ill or suffer injuries and it doesn't matter whether or not they are caused by the work they do. What is important is that they receive immediate attention and that an ambulance is called for in serious cases.

Table 8.5 Audit for first aid

Date	Name of early years setting			Name of auditor	
		Yes	No	N/A	Comments
1	There is an appointed person available to take charge of first aid arrangements				
2	There is a suitably stocked first aid box				
3	Records are kept of all accidents and emergencies				
4	The local emergency services have been provided with the location of the early years setting				
5	The appointed person has undertaken an emergency first aid training course including first aid for children				
6	All first-aiders have undertaken a paediatric first aid training course				
7	First aid provision is reviewed annually				
8	First aid notices including names of first-aiders or appointed person on duty are displayed appropriately in the premises				
9	First aid is included in staff induction and annual updates				
10	Specific first aid hazards have been identified in the assessment process				
11	First aid at work certificates are current and up to date				
12	All first aid boxes are marked with a white cross on a green background				
13	Travelling first aid boxes are available for off-site activities				
14	Personal protective equipment of disposable gloves and aprons is provided				
15	Hand washing facilities are available				

It is the decision of the employer as to what is considered to be appropriate and adequate for their workplace and they have to assess what their first aid needs are.

First aid provision (Table 8.6)

The minimum first aid provision is:

- a suitably stocked first aid box specifically for treating children;
- an appointed person to take charge of first aid arrangements;
- information for employees on first aid arrangements;
- a qualified paediatric first-aider on duty at all times when children are present, whether in the setting or on an outing;
- a record of accidents and first aid treatments given.

The *Management of Health and Safety at Work Regulations (HSE) 1992* require employers to undertake a suitable and sufficient assessment of the risks to the health and safety of their employees at work. The first aid needs should be reviewed regularly, at least annually, especially if there have been any changes, to make sure that the provision is adequate.

All staff must be informed of the first aid arrangements within the early years setting. This can be achieved by:

- displaying first aid notices stating the location of equipment, facilities, names of first aid personnel and the procedures for monitoring and reviewing the early years setting's needs;
- displaying the notices in a prominent place throughout the early years setting, at least one in each building if the nursery is on several sites;
- including first aid information in induction programmes for new staff and in staff handbooks and information for parents.

Staff should hold an appropriate first aid certificate in paediatric first aid. To meet the EYFS, paediatric first aid courses must be approved by the local authority where the early years setting is situated and comply with the criteria described in the *Practice Guidance for the Early Years Foundation Stage* (2008).

What is an appointed person?

An appointed person is someone who is chosen to:

- take charge when someone is injured or ill, including calling an ambulance if needed;
- look after first aid equipment, checking that the contents are correct, in working order and in date.

Appointed persons should not try to give first aid for which they have not been trained and should undertake refresher courses to maintain their skills. Paediatric first aid courses meet the following criteria:

Table 8.6 Assessment of first aid provision

Points to consider	Action to take
What are the significant risks in your workplace? What are the risks of injury or ill health? Are there any specific risks, such as working with hazardous substances?	– Specific training for first-aiders – Extra first aid treatment – Precise placing of first aid equipment
What is your record of accidents and cases of ill health? What type are they and where did they happen?	– Make provision in certain areas depending upon records of past accidents – Review the contents of the first aid box
How many staff are employed?	A qualified paediatric first-aider must be available in the setting at all times when children are present
Are there inexperienced staff on the site or employees with disabilities or special health problems?	– Special equipment – Local siting of equipment
What is the size of the early years setting? Is it on split sites or levels?	Consider additional provision for first aid in each building or on each floor
Is there shift work or out of hours working?	First aid provision has to be available at all times people are at work
Is the early years setting remote from the local emergency services?	It is good practice to inform the local emergency services, in writing, of the location of the premises (with Ordinance Survey grid references if necessary) and information that might affect access to the premises. If there is more than one entrance, clear instructions should be given as to where or to whom they should report.
Are there any work experience trainees?	First aid provision covers all those on the premises as well as children and staff.

- planning and managing emergencies;
- cardiopulmonary resuscitation appropriate to the age of the child;
- recognising different causes of shock and how to manage each appropriately;
- recognise and manage bleeding;
- recognise and manage burns and scalds injuries;
- recognise and manage choking injuries;
- manage suspected fractures appropriately;
- manage suspected head, neck and back injuries appropriately;
- recognise and manage suspected cases of poisoning appropriately;
- manage foreign bodies in eyes, ears and noses appropriately;
- manage eye injuries appropriately;

- manage bites and stings appropriately;
- manage suspected cases caused by extremes of heat and cold resulting in heat exhaustion and hypothermia;
- manage seizures and febrile convulsions appropriately;
- recognise and manage children with chronic medical conditions including epilepsy, asthma, diabetes and sickle cell anaemia appropriately;
- recognise and manage sudden serious illnesses such as meningitis appropriately.

Emergency first aid training should help an appointed person to cope with an emergency, improving their competence and confidence. It may be necessary to appoint more than one person to this role to cover the working hours of the premises.

What is a first-aider?

A first-aider is someone who has undergone training to provide first aid at work and has a current First Aid at Work certificate. Local authorities require that the course leads to a certificate for a minimum of 12 hours that is recognised and approved by the Health and Safety Executive (HSE) or by an awarding body such as Ofqual in England (Office of Qualifications and Examinations Regulation), the Scottish Qualifications Authority, and DCELLS (Department for Children, Education and Lifelong Skills) in Wales.

It is important that any training organisation is informed of the ages of children that are cared for so that appropriate training can be given as the requirements are very different from those for adults, especially in resuscitation.

The main duties of a first-aider are to:

- give immediate help to those with common injuries or illnesses and those arising from specific hazards in the early years setting;
- make sure that an ambulance or other professional medical help is called when necessary.

Unless it is part of their contract of employment, staff agreeing to become first-aiders do so on a voluntary basis. When selecting someone to undertake the role of first-aider, you should consider:

- reliability and communication skills;
- aptitude and ability to absorb new knowledge and learn new skills;
- ability to cope with stressful and physically demanding emergency procedures;
- normal duties – they must be able to leave immediately to attend to an emergency.

The minimum requirement is that an appointed person must take charge of the first aid arrangements, and the number of appointed persons needed has to be decided by the employer, following the risk assessment. Cover must be available at all times that people are on the premises.

Employers should make sure that their insurance arrangements provide full cover for claims arising from staff acting within the scope of their employment. Those early years settings that come under the local authority should consult with them about their insurance arrangements.

Keeping qualifications up to date

First-aiders must hold a valid certificate of competence issued by an organisation approved by the HSE.

- First Aid at Work and Emergency First Aid at Work certificates are valid for three years.
- Employers should arrange refresher courses and refreshing of competence before certificates expire; these are usually annually.
- If an individual's certificate expires they will have to undertake another full course.
- Refresher courses can be arranged up to three months before the expiry date and the new certificate takes effect from the date of expiry.
- Early years settings should keep a record of first-aiders and certification dates.

First aid materials, equipment and facilities

Employers must provide proper materials, equipment and facilities at all times. First aid equipment must be clearly labelled and easily accessible.

First aid containers

- There should be at least one fully stocked first aid container for each setting. The assessment should include the number of first aid containers.
- Additional first aid containers will be needed for split sites, high risk areas and any off-site activities such as outings.
- All first aid containers must be marked with a white cross on a green background.
- Where you place first aid containers should be given careful consideration – if possible they should be kept near to hand washing facilities.
- All staff should know where the first aid box is placed and it should be clearly visible and marked.

Contents of a first aid container

There is no set list of items to keep in a first aid box as it depends upon how needs are assessed. The HSE recommends a minimum stock of first aid items should include:

- a leaflet giving general guidance on first aid;
- 20 individually wrapped sterile adhesive dressings (assorted sizes);
- two sterile eye pads;
- four individually wrapped triangular bandages (preferably sterile);
- six safety pins;
- six medium sized (12 cm x 12 cm) individually wrapped sterile unmedicated wound dressings;
- two large (18 cm x 18 cm) sterile individually wrapped unmedicated wound dressings;
- one pair of disposable gloves.

Other equipment that is appropriate for the setting should be kept nearby and can include:

- disposable plastic aprons;
- scissors;
- eye protection;
- spillage kit for body fluids.

Tablets and medicines must not be kept in the first aid box.

The first aid procedures should identify the person responsible for maintaining the contents of the container, which should be checked frequently and restocked after use. Keep a record sheet to be signed each time the kit is checked and restocked.

Travelling first aid containers

A first aid container should be provided for off-site visits and the manager should assess the level of first aid provision needed. The HSE recommends that where there is no special risk identified a minimum stock of first aid items for travelling first aid containers is:

- a leaflet giving general advice on first aid;
- six individually wrapped sterile adhesive dressings;
- one large sterile unmedicated wound dressing (18 cm x 18 cm);
- two triangular bandages;
- two safety pins;
- individually wrapped moist cleansing wipes;
- one pair of disposable gloves.

Other useful items to include and carry are:

- bottled sterile water;
- soap and water cleansing wipes.

Transport regulations

Transport regulations require that all minibuses and public service vehicles used have on board a first aid container with the following items:

- ten antiseptic wipes, foil packaged;
- one conforming disposable bandage (not less than 7.5 cm wide);
- two triangular bandages;
- one packet of 24 assorted adhesive dressings;
- three large sterile unmedicated ambulance dressings (not less than 15 cm x 20 cm);
- two sterile eye pads with attachments;
- 12 assorted safety pins;
- one pair of rustless blunt-ended scissors.

The first aid container has to be:

- maintained in a good condition;
- suitable for the purpose of keeping the items in a good condition (i.e. rust-proof, dust-proof and damp-proof);
- readily available for use;
- marked as a first aid container.

Infection control precautions

All staff should take precautions to prevent infection and follow basic hygiene procedures. Personal protective equipment should be provided, which includes the use of single-use disposable gloves and plastic aprons when handling blood or body fluids. Hand washing facilities should be easily accessible and used dressings and bandages should be disposed of safely as clinical waste.

First aid records

It is a legal requirement to keep records of accidents at work in a book of any incidents involving injuries or illness which have happened. Any information recorded must comply with the *Data Protection Act 1998* and managers should be aware of the *Freedom of Information Act 2000 for England, Wales and Northern Ireland* and the *Freedom of Information (Scotland) Act 2002* which affect all public authorities.

The following information should be recorded:

- date, time and place of injury;
- name and job role of injured or ill person;
- details of injury/illness and any first aid given;
- what happened to the casualty immediately afterwards (went home/hospital etc.);
- name and signature of the person who dealt with the incident.

Reporting accidents

Certain accidents must be reported to the HSE including those of physical violence to staff and accidents to people who are not at work, which includes accidents to children.

Employers who have ten or more members of staff must keep readily accessible records in either a written or electronic format for a minimum of three years. Where the local authority is the employer, the early years setting should follow their local authority procedures as they may wish you to report directly to them centrally for insurance or statistical purposes.

Early years settings must inform Ofsted of the following within 14 days:

- an outbreak of infectious disease that is considered sufficiently serious by a registered medical practitioner;
- any serious injury to, or a serious illness or death of, any child or other person on the premises;

- any allegations of serious harm against, or abuse of, a child by any person looking after children, or living, working or employed at the premises;
- any serious matter or event that is likely to affect the welfare of any child on the premises.

Under the *Reporting of Injuries, Diseases and Dangerous Occurrences Regulations 1995* some accidents must be reported to the HSE. Fatal and major injuries and dangerous occurrences must be notified immediately (e.g. by telephone) and followed up within ten days with a written report. Other incidents must be reported to the HSE within ten days. It is important to remember that for most employers a reportable accident, dangerous occurrence or case of disease is a comparatively rare event. It is, however, a legal requirement to report it when it does occur.

Workplace violence and personal safety

It is good practice to have a general policy on workplace violence that includes ways to minimise its occurrence. It should include:

- staff training;
- the working environment;
- maintenance of adequate staffing levels;
- back-up procedures for emergencies.

Training should include:

- personal safety training;
- recognising signs that could lead to aggressive behaviour;
- using techniques to calm situations and potential assailants.

Types of incidents include:

- *assault* – any intentional or reckless act that causes someone to fear or expect immediate unlawful force or personal violence;
- *battery* – the intentional or reckless infliction of unlawful force or personal violence.

The two offences may occur together and, in all but minor cases, early years settings should refer any assaults that appear to involve actual bodily harm to the police.

Legal requirements

- Identify all hazards to children, both indoors and outdoors, and keep to a minimum.
- Conduct a risk assessment and review it at least annually.
- Comply with all health and safety legislation.
- Comply with fire safety regulations.
- Have at least one person with a current paediatric first aid certificate on the premises whenever children are present.

Best practice checklist

- Have a health and safety plan.
- Always consider health and safety before any new activity is started.
- Identify all hazards in the workplace and assess risks to staff, children and visitors.
- Have emergency plans and practice evacuation procedures.
- Provide training for staff on all aspects of health and safety, both on starting work and in annual updates.
- Standards put in place should be reviewed and updated regularly.

Self review activity

Using one of the audit tables within this chapter, look around your area of work and consider whether you have similar measures in place.

Discuss your findings with colleagues and decide whether the audit tool needs to be adapted to reflect your premises' activities and how you answered the questions. Does it identify gaps in staff knowledge and do policies need to be reviewed and updated?

Summary

This chapter has reviewed the different subject areas to be included in a health and safety policy. Having a written policy is never enough; it is important to be able to measure whether the precautions you have implemented have been successful. Such monitoring should be an active process that does not rely upon reacting to accidents or to occasions when things go wrong. Undertaking audits by yourself or using outside agencies tells you about the reliability and effectiveness of your systems.

Bibliography

Bilton, H. (2004) *Playing Outside: Activities, Ideas and Inspiration for the Early Years.* London: David Fulton Publishers.

British Standard EN 1176 (1997) *The European Standard for Playground Equipment.* London: TSO.

British Standard EN 1177 (1997) *The European Standard for Impact Absorbing Playground Surfacing: Safety Requirements and Test Methods.* London: TSO.

British Standard 1722 (2006) *BS 1722 Part 5: Specification for Close Board and Wooden Palisade Fences.* London: TSO.

Child Accident Prevention Trust (CAPT) (2003) *Preventing Childhood Accidents: Guidance on Effective Action.* London: CAPT. Available at http://www.capt.org.uk [accessed 26th April 2011].

Child Accident Prevention Trust (CAPT) (2004a) *Safety in Day Care and Play Settings.* London: CAPT. Available at http://www.capt.org.uk [accessed 26th April 2011].

Child Accident Prevention Trust (CAPT) (2004b) *Toys and Accidents Factsheet.* London: CAPT. Available at http://www.capt.org.uk [accessed 26th April 2011].

The Childcare Act 2006. London: TSO.

Data Protection Act 1998. London: TSO.

Department for Children, Schools and Families (2008) *Statutory Framework for the Early Years Foundation Stage.* Nottingham, UK: DCSF Publications.

Department for Children, Schools and Families (2008) *Practice Guidance for the Early Years Foundation Stage.* Nottingham, UK: DCSF Publications.

Department for Children, Schools and Families (2009) *The Childcare (Disqualification) Regulations 2009.* London: TSO.

Department for Education and Employment (1996) *Education (School Premises) Regulations 1996.* London: TSO.

Department for Education and Skills (1998) *Health and Safety of Pupils on Educational Visits: A Good Practice Guide (HASPV2).* Available at https://www.education.gov.uk/publications/standard/publicationdetail/page1/HSPV2 [accessed 6th July 2011].

Department of Trade and Industry (1995) *Toys (Safety) Regulations 1995* (Statutory Instrument 1995/204). London: TSO. Available at http://www.bis.gov.uk/files/file11286.pdf [accessed 26th April 2011].

Department of Trade and Industry (1999) *Consumer Safety Research: Burns and Scalds Accidents in the Home.* London: TSO.

Employers' Liability (Compulsory Insurance) Act 1969. London: TSO.

The Food Hygiene (England) Regulations 2006. London: TSO.

The Food Hygiene (Scotland) Regulations 2006. London: TSO.

The Food Hygiene (Wales) Regulations 2006. London: TSO.

The Food Hygiene (Northern Ireland) Regulations 2006. London: TSO.

The Food Safety Act 1990 (Amendment) Regulations 2004. London: TSO.

Freedom of Information Act 2000 for England, Wales and Northern Ireland. London: TSO.

Freedom of Information (Scotland) Act 2002. London: TSO.

Health and Safety at Work etc. Act 1974. London: TSO.

Health Protection Agency (2010) *Avoiding Infection on Farm Visits.* HPA: London.

Health and Safety Commission (1981) *Health and Safety (First Aid) Regulations 1981.* London: TSO.

Health and Safety Commission (1989) *Electricity at Work Regulations 1989.* London: TSO.

Health and Safety Commission (1989) *Health and Safety Information for Employees Regulations 1989.* London: TSO.

Health and Safety Commission (1989) *Noise at Work Regulations 1989.* London: TSO.

Health and Safety Commission (1992) *Health and Safety (Display Screen Equipment) Regulations 1992 (amended 2002).* London: TSO.

Health and Safety Commission (1992) *Manual Handling Operations Regulations 1992 (Amended 2002).* London: TSO.

Health and Safety Commission (1992) *Personal Protective Equipment at Work Regulations 1992.* London: TSO.

Health and Safety Commission (1998) *Provision and Use of Work Equipment Regulations 1998.* London: TSO.

Health and Safety Executive (HSE) (1992) *Workplace (Health, Safety and Welfare) Regulations 1992.* London: TSO.

Health and Safety Executive (HSE) (1995) *The Reporting of Injuries, Diseases and Dangerous Occurrences Regulations.* London: The Stationery Office.

Health and Safety Executive (HSE) (1997) *Fire Precautions (Workplace) Regulations 1997.* London: TSO.

Health and Safety Executive (HSE) (1997) *First Aid at Work – Approved code of Practice and Guidance Revised 1997.* London: TSO.

Health and Safety Executive (HSE) (1999) *Management of Health and Safety at Work Regulations 1999.* London: TSO.

Health and Safety Executive (2000) *Avoiding Ill Health at Open Farms – Advice to Farmers and Teachers.* (AIS23 Supplement (revised)). Sudbury: HSE. Available at http://www.hse.gov.uk/pubns/ais23.pdf [accessed 26th April 2011].

Health and Safety Executive (HSE) (2002) *Control of Substances Hazardous to Health (COSHH) (Amendments) Regulations 2002.* London: HSE Books.

Health and Safety Executive (HSE) (2003) *The Management of Health and Safety at Work and Fire Precautions (Workplace) (Amendment) Regulations 2003.* London: TSO.

Health and Safety Executive (HSE) (2009) *The Health and Safety Law Poster.* London: HSE Books.

Health and Safety Executive (HSE)/Local Authorities Enforcement Liaison Committee (HELA) (2002) Local Authority Circular (LAC 79/2) *Safety in Children's Playgrounds.* Sudbury: HSE.

Mathers, S. and Linskey, F. (2009) UK Addendum April 2009 to Harms, T., Clifford, R. M., Cryer, D. (1998) The Early Childhood Environment Rating Scale (ECERS-S). Available at http://www.ecersuk.org [accessed 2nd July 2011].

Maxwell, R. (1984) Quality assessment in health. *British Medical Journal,* vol 288: pp 1470–2.

Regulatory Reform (Fire Safety) Order 2005. London: TSO.

Royal Horticultural Society (2004) *Potentially Harmful Garden Safety Checklist.* Surrey: RHS. Available at http://www.rhs.org.uk/Gardening/Sustainable-gardening/pdfs/c_and_e_harmful [accessed 26th April 2011].

Royal Society for the Prevention of Accidents (2004) Information sheet number 20. *Fencing for Children's Play Areas.*

Royal Society for the Prevention of Accidents. *Home and Garden Safety Checklist.* Available at http://www.rospa.com/homesafety/Info/home-garden-safety-checklist.pdf [accessed 26th April 2011].

Royal Society for the Prevention of Accidents. *The Toy Safety Code.* Available at http://www.rospa.com/childsafety/atplay/default.aspx [accessed 2nd July 2011].